Teach®
Yourself

The Writer's Guide to Good Style

A practical guide for twenty-first century writers

Katherine Lapworth

Hodder Education

338 Euston Road, London NW1 3BH.

Hodder Education is an Hachette UK company

First published in UK 2011 by Hodder Education

First published in US 2011 by The McGraw-Hill Companies, Inc.

This edition published 2011.

British Library Cataloguing in Publication Data: a catalogue record for this title is available from the British Library.

Library of Congress Catalog Card Number: on file.

10 9 8 7 6 5 4 3 2 1

The publisher has used its best endeavours to ensure that any website addresses referred to in this book are correct and active at the time of going to press. However, the publisher and the author have no responsibility for the websites and can make no guarantee that a site will remain live or that the content will remain relevant, decent or appropriate.

The publisher has made every effort to mark as such all words which it believes to be trademarks. The publisher should also like to make it clear that the presence of a word in the book, whether marked or unmarked, in no way affects its legal status as a trademark.

Every reasonable effort has been made by the publisher to trace the copyright holders of material in this book. Any errors or omissions should be notified in writing to the publisher, who will endeavour to rectify the situation for any reprints and future editions.

Hachette UK's policy is to use papers that are natural, renewable and recyclable products and made from wood grown in sustainable forests. The logging and manufacturing processes are expected to conform to the environmental regulations of the country of origin.

www.hoddereducation.co.uk

Typeset by Cenveo Publisher Services.

Printed and bound by CPI Group (UK) Ltd, Croydon, CR0 4YY

Also available in ebook

Contents

About this book

Welcome to *The Writer's Guide to Good Style: A practical guide for twenty-first century writers*.

Not so long ago, it seems, people were worrying about the demise of writing. Mobile phones and texting, the doom-sayers predicted, would finish off grammar and punctuation. The writing was on the wall for writing.

In fact, the opposite has happened. We are now writing more than ever before. We send emails and texts, we comment on blogs, keep in touch with friends on social networking sites, as well as write reports, letters and presentations as we did before. A day doesn't go by when we don't write something.

Writing is all about communication. To do that successfully means knowing who your reader is and getting your message across so that the reader understands what you are trying to say. And for that, you need to know the basic rules of punctuation and grammar. You also have to appreciate that fashions change (even in writing). Some rules can be bent, some should never have been rules in the first place and some are carved in stone and shouldn't be messed with.

A good writing style is the way in which a writer uses the English language to express themselves. Every time you write something, you will be judged on what you have written. This book will help you to improve your style and become a better writer.

In one minute

Style is the way in which writers use language to express themselves. Some writers are masters at this; the rest of us just want to write a clear, coherent style of English to get by in our daily lives.

In this book, we will look at what you need to be able to write clearly and concisely in the twenty-first century. You can use the whole book or concentrate on the chapters which deal with the areas you feel need most work.

Good grammar is the foundation of a good writing style. Chapter 1 looks at grammar; it will help you identify what goes into a sentence and explain the rules that will help you communicate clearly.

Punctuation helps give the tone of voice to a piece and it organizes the grammar so the reader understands the words. Chapter 2 looks at the art of punctuation.

Chapter 3 deals with presentation – how your writing looks on the page. Chapter 4 concentrates on writing with your reader in mind. Chapter 5 looks at what not to do – the things to avoid that can confuse or annoy readers.

The next three chapters look at particular types of writing. 'Business' writing is any writing people do at work or as an individual. We deal with letter writing in Chapter 7 and concentrate on electronic communication (emails, blogs, tweets, texts and web pages) in Chapter 8.

The final chapter aims to help you become a better writer. Writing is a craft and one that can be learned and improved on.

1

Introduction and grammar

In this chapter you will learn about:
- **nouns, pronouns and adjectives**
- **verbs, tenses and adverbs**
- **conjunctions, prepositions and determiners**
- **subjects and objects.**

> *A good style should show no sign of effort. What is written should seem a happy accident.*
>
> Somerset Maugham

Introduction

You don't need to be a published author to call yourself a writer these days. We are all writers; it's almost impossible *not* to write. From emails to texts, writing a 'thank you' letter or a job application, we communicate with each other by writing.

Style is the way in which writers use language to express themselves. For some writers, their style is exceptional, able to move us with the way they use their words. The rest of us are just hoping to write a clear, intelligible style of English to get by in our daily lives.

As with most things in life, usage and fashion change how we do things. Writing styles are no different; English is a living language that changes and adapts all the time. Within those shifting patterns and trends, there are rules and guidelines that help keep the language under control so that we can communicate successfully with each other. These are the rules of grammar and punctuation. If you don't know how grammar and punctuation work, you appear ignorant to others. Though it may seem unfair, people judge us by the way we write and speak as much as how we look and sound or the clothes we wear or the house we live in.

In this book, we will look at the different types of writing we need to do in our daily lives. We will cover areas where people often struggle with rules and usage and we will discuss ways in which we can become better writers.

> ### Did you know?
> Charlotte Bronte's school report of 1825 said 'She knows nothing of grammar' and remarked that she could only write 'indifferently'.

> **Important note:** The eagle-eyed among you will notice that some of the style suggestions mentioned here are not actually reflected in this book and that is because the publisher, Hodder Education, has its own particular house style when it comes to producing *Teach Yourself* books. One is not 'more correct' than the other; they are the preferred way of doing something. Just as one person might have short hair and another chooses to leave theirs long, most publishers, publications and companies have an individual house style that gives them their identity and sets them slightly apart from one another.

Grammar – a short history

It is difficult to avoid mentioning Latin when discussing grammar. In Medieval times, educated people wrote in Latin and, in those days, 'grammar' meant the study of Latin. Nowadays, grammar is the study of language in general in which there is a set of standards or a system of rules that we follow to show that we can speak and write correctly.

Books on English grammar and style guides have been produced since the 1500s but it wasn't until the eighteenth century that the rules governing English grammar became really restrictive. *A Short Introduction to English Grammar* was one of the most influential books in Britain, written by an Oxford academic, Robert Lowth, in 1762. Unfortunately, a lot of those rules were taken from Latin. As a written 'dead' language (rather than a living, spoken one), Latin had lots of established rules that never changed and which gave order and precision. And it worked well – for Latin. It was quite a different matter with English, a living language. Many of the difficulties that people subsequently have had with learning (and understanding) the rules of grammar have occured because the union of the English language (with its Germanic base) with the concepts of Latin and Greek grammar did not always work well together.

This was not a problem while the vast majority of the population did not read or write. But when schooling became compulsory in the second half of the nineteenth century, all children had to learn grammar.

Did you know?

The following is a poem written for Victorian schoolchildren.

The Nine Articles of Speech

Three little words we often see,
Determiners, like *a*, *an* and *the*.

A **noun**'s the name of anything,
As *school* or *garden*, *hoop* or *string*.

An **adjective** tells the kind of noun,
As *great*, *small*, *pretty*, *white* or *brown*.

Instead of nouns the **pronouns** stand,
John's head, *his* face, *my* arm, *your* hand.

Verbs tell of something being done,
To *read*, *write*, *count*, *sing*, *jump* or *run*.

How things are done, the **adverbs** tell,
Like *slowly*, *quickly*, *ill* or *well*.

A **preposition** stands before
A noun, as *in* a room or *through* a door.

Conjunctions join the nouns together,
Like boy *or* girl, wind *and* weather.

The **interjection** shows surprise,
Like *Oh!* How charming. *Ah!* How wise.

The whole are called 'nine parts of speech',
Which reading, writing and speaking, teach.

John Neale (1886)

Generations of school children had to learn the rules of grammar whether they liked it or not. At least they knew how to punctuate, spell and write a coherent sentence. Then, in the second half of the twentieth century, there was a period of about twenty-five to thirty years where the teaching of grammar was considered unnecessary in schools. The result of that was huge numbers of people entering higher education and the working world with an inadequate knowledge of how to write correctly.

Good grammar does not automatically guarantee you a great writing style. That comes from your choice of words, how you put them together and the originality of your thoughts and ideas. However, good grammar is the foundation of good style; it's the framework that you build your style on and grammar is what we will start with in this chapter.

Grammar – the rules

If you speak English, you already have a basic grasp of grammar. You may not know *about* it but you know what sounds good and when something doesn't sound quite right; that is, when the pattern of words hits a wrong note. One of your strongest weapons as a writer is a good ear. Listen in your head to what you have written or others have written. Does it flow and make sense? If it doesn't, there is usually a problem with the grammar.

Grammar is the system and structure of a language. There is a standard way of using grammar that you find in newspapers, magazines, official documents and books. Non-standard use can be found in slang, dialect, very informal communications between friends and people who just don't know how to use grammar correctly. Your friends may not wince if you use a double negative or mix your tenses but others will. Good English needs good grammar.

CLAUSES

We refer to 'clauses' in this book. A clause is not necessarily a whole sentence but it does contain at least a verb and a subject and other related words that give information about the subject. It is the smallest grammatical unit that can express a complete proposition (proposition = meaning).

4

Clause = subject + verb. If there is no verb or subject, there is no clause. A sentence should contain at least one clause. For example:

The book, which was written at the turn of the century, was a best-seller as soon as it was published.

▶ The **main, independent** clause – 'The book was a best-seller as soon as it was published' – can stand on its own.
▶ The **dependent, subordinate** clause – The book 'which was written at the turn of the century' – relies on the other clause.

NOUNS

The traditional definition of a noun has been that it is the name of a person, place or thing. 'Thing' is a rather vague term that covers anything from 'chair' to 'beauty'. There are three types of nouns:

▶ **ordinary or 'common' nouns** – (butter, eggs, horses, chairs, shoes, pencil, table).
▶ **proper nouns** – names of specific people, places, times, occasions, events or publications, etc.; they start with a capital letter (Katherine, Prince Philip, London, Tuesday, Easter, The Times).
▶ **abstract nouns** – names of things you can't physically touch or see (direction, poverty, beauty, hope, faith).

Plural nouns
Most nouns, when they are plural, have an 's' on the end (for example, *cats*, *trees*, *tables*).

▶ Those ending in 's', 'x', 'ch', 'sh' need '-es' to make them plural (for example, box – boxes, switch – switches).
▶ Those ending in '-y' but where the letter before it is not a vowel, the '-y' becomes '-ies' (for example, city – cities, lorry – lorries).
▶ Irregular plurals (those that don't follow the usual pattern) do not need an 's' added (for example, child – children, mouse – mice, sheep – sheep, ox – oxen, wife – wives, man – men, loaf – loaves, foot – feet).
▶ Proper nouns tend to be singular (London, not Londons) unlike ordinary nouns (hat – hats); they are not usually used with determiners such as 'a', 'the', 'some', etc. and are written with a capital letter.

A single subject/noun takes the single form of the verb; plural subjects take the plural form of the verb. When two nouns are linked as the subject of the sentence, you often have a choice of whether you use the single or plural form of the verb. It depends on the two nouns because some can be seen as a single entity or idea (such as *law and order*; *gin and tonic*).

Collective nouns

Collective nouns are names for a group of things (such as: *family, audience, squad, team, enemy, board, band*, a *flock* of sheep, a *pride* of lions, etc.). A collective noun effectively creates a single entity which, although it is describing more than one thing (*audience* = a group of people), tends to be treated as a single noun. Therefore, the 'team *is* boarding the plane' rather than the 'team *are* boarding the plane'. There can be problems with collective nouns if you are not sure whether they should be regarded as singular or plural. We will look at this in more detail in Chapter 5.

SOME UNUSUAL COLLECTIVE NOUNS
- ▶ A clamour of rooks
- ▶ A murder of crows
- ▶ An exultation of larks
- ▶ A knot of toads
- ▶ A chattering of starlings
- ▶ An ostentation of peacocks
- ▶ A parliament of owls.

Insight

If a noun is used to qualify another, then the first noun is usually in the singular ('six-inch holes' rather than 'six-inches holes').

PRONOUNS

These are words that stand in for a noun, often to avoid repeating a word (Janice, *who* dances, was busy rehearsing when the teacher told *her* to stay behind after class.).

A pronoun can be a person, place, idea or thing.

- ▶ **personal** (singular or plural) – I, you, he, she, it, we, they
- ▶ **reflexive** – myself, yourself, ourselves, itself
- ▶ **possessive** (who owns what) – my, your, his, ours, theirs, its, mine
- ▶ **reciprocal** – each other, one another
- ▶ **relative** – who, whom, what, which, that (to link clauses)
- ▶ **interrogative** (asking questions) – who, when, whose, which, what

- ▶ **demonstrative** – this/these, that/those
- ▶ **indefinite** – each, both, either, all, any, someone, few, some, many, most, more.

Pronouns can be the subject or the object of a sentence: '*I* am the subject of the sentence' (subject) but 'The sentence is about *me*' (object).

Insight

'It' is an extremely flexible pronoun: it can be both a subject and an object pronoun which you can use to refer to different parts of a sentence.

Problems can arise when the sentence has two subjects: for example, Alice and *me*...or should that be Alice and *I*? To make sure you get the right pronoun, find the subject, and ask yourself who or what is doing the action of the verb in a sentence:

- ▶ Alice and me are going on holiday. – Wrong

Split the sentence up: Alice is going on holiday; *me* is going on holiday. *Me* is not a subject pronoun but *I* is. Therefore, change '*me*' to '*I*':

- ▶ Alice and I are going on holiday. – Correct

Numbers can also act as pronouns: 'We got up at *six* in the morning and managed to be *first* in the queue.'

ADJECTIVES

Adjectives are words that qualify (or describe) a number, colour, type or other qualities of a noun or pronoun:

- ▶ He lived in a small house with a red door.
- ▶ It was an exciting trip.

Most adjectives have three forms:

1 positive (big, happy)
2 comparative (bigger, happier)
3 superlative (biggest, happiest).

Adjectives usually come before nouns but not always (as in 'The house is *small* and the door is *red*.'). They can sometimes function as a noun ('The *old* and the *infirm*') or as an adverb ('a *quick*-witted girl', 'a *bitter*-cold night').

You can have several adjectives in a clause or sentence and there is no hard and fast rule as to the order they should be written in. It is a case of using common sense and what sounds best. For example, which of the following sounds better?

▶ On holiday, we visited the beautiful, ancient stone castles and palaces.
▶ On holiday, we visited the stone, ancient, beautiful castles and palaces.

The first makes more sense even though all the words in both sentences are the same. The order is the only thing that is different. Remember that the more natural and logical the sequence of adjectives, the more likely the reader is to understand the sentence and absorb the information.

ADVERBS

Adverbs add colour and meaning to a verb, an adjective or another adverb. They tell us how, where or when a verb happens (for example, 'she talked *loudly*'). When an adverb is directly linked to the verb so that it describes how the action is being done, as in the above example, it is called a *modifying* adverb ('loudly' modifies the verb 'talked').

▶ The position of adverbs in a sentence is flexible; they do not have to come after a verb. For example:
  ▷ We walked slowly; I quickly ran; the steak is well cooked.
▶ Adverbs can be one word or several. They give us an idea of a whole range of meanings such as how something is done, where it is being done and when. For example:
  ▷ We remained happily / at home / that weekend.
  ▷ David missed the bus and had to walk a long way.
▶ Adverbs can work together as adverb phrases. If you find that you have several together, it is usual to put them in the following order: how, where, when. In other words:
  ▷ We will meet as soon as possible (how) at head office (where) next week (when).

Some words can be either an adjective or an adverb, depending on where they are in a sentence. They look the same but take their role as one or the other from the way they function in the sentence.

Adjectives: They took the *early* train; it was *late* morning; we had a *fine* room.

Adverbs: They arrived *early*; we started *late*; she seemed *fine*.

Generally, many (but not all) adverbs end in -ly (*slowly, pleasantly, gently, generally*) but not all words ending in -ly are adverbs (for example, '*kindly*' and '*deadly*' are adjectives).

Insight

Resist the urge to use adverbs at every opportunity. When you review your writing, check how many adverbs you have used and see if you can replace them with a different verb. For example: change 'I eat my food *quickly*' to 'I gobble my food'. Substitute 'I ran *slowly*' for 'I jogged'.

CONJUNCTIONS

Conjunctions are joining words; they link words, sentences and parts of sentences (clauses) together.

▶ I wrote a note but forgot to leave it because I was in a hurry.

The different kinds of conjunctions are:

▶ **co-ordinating** – linking words/phrases of equal importance: 'The road is long *and* hard.'
▶ **subordinating** – linking less important phrases to one or more of greater importance: 'I used to play tennis *when* I was a girl.'

Examples of conjunctions:

and	because	but	or	nor
yet	so	although	for	when

PREPOSITIONS

These are probably some of the shortest words in the English language but they play an important part in a sentence despite their small size. They come before nouns and pronouns ('preposition' means 'something that is placed before') and help give meaning or connection between two parts of a sentence. They are joining words and do not work on their own; they are always with an object.

▶ We started to leave *at* midday.
▶ She lived *in* an apartment.
▶ The books are *on* the table.
▶ We travelled *through* the night *on* a train.

Examples of prepositions:

about	by	because of	on	through
across	down	in terms of	onto	to
after	apart from	inside	out	near to
at	in spite of	into	over	toward/s
ahead of	during	of	instead of	under
as far as	for	off	with reference to	up
before	from	due to	round	with
behind	in	on behalf of	since	

DETERMINERS AND ARTICLES

Determiners go before nouns and noun phrases. The most common are:

- ▶ the – definite article, used to identify a specific (or definite) thing:
  - ▷ The dog chases the ball (it is a known dog chasing a particular ball).
- ▶ a / an* – indefinite article, referring to singular nouns in general:
  - ▷ I must buy a ball (any ball will do, it doesn't have to be a particular one).

*Use 'a' when a word starts with a hard 'h' ('a hand') and use 'an' when a word starts with a silent 'h' ('an hour'). Pronouns and proper nouns do not need articles.

Determiners allow us to express many distinctions of quantity (*some* people), emotion (*what* beauty), ask questions (*where* is it?) and possession (*your* books). Like adjectives, they only make sense when attached to a noun or a noun phrase.

Numbers also act as determiners (*two* dogs, *seven* countries). There are three types of number:

- ▶ **cardinal** – e.g. 4, four, 89, eighty-nine, three hundred, million
- ▶ **ordinal** – e.g. third, eleventh, 45th
- ▶ **fractions** – e.g. third, half, three-sixths.

Numbers – singular or plural?

- ▶ If you are talking about a specific number, 'the number twenty-five', then it is treated as a singular noun and therefore needs a single verb ('the number is 25').

▶ If you are talking about a number of things, then this means that you have plural nouns which need plural verbs ('a number of trains were delayed').

Expressions that use numbers can be either singular or plural. It depends on the context of the sentence and whether you are using them as a single entity or as individual entities in a group. For example:

▶ 13.1 miles is a half marathon and a long way to run (it's a single distance).
▶ The 13 miles are uphill all the way (every one of the thirteen miles goes uphill so plural).

We will discuss numbers and how to write with them in greater detail in Chapter 3.

VERBS

Practically every sentence needs a verb. A verb is the 'doing' or 'state of being' word that the meaning of the sentence rests on. It is generally one word but you can have multi-word verbs, such as *sit down, come in, get off, look down on* (these are called phrasal verbs). The verb you choose to use determines what other grammatical elements you can have in a clause. You can break them down into different types.

REGULAR VERBS
Regular verbs follow a pattern so you can predict the form the verb is going to take depending on whether it's singular or plural (I *eat*, you *eat*, he/she *eats*, we *eat*, you *eat*, they *eat*).

IRREGULAR VERBS
Some forms of verb are unpredictable. Luckily there aren't huge numbers of irregular verbs. The best known is probably 'to be' (I *am*, you *are*, he/she *is*, we *are*, you *are*, they *are*).

TRANSITIVE VERBS
This is where a subject does something to a direct object, e.g. 'We *caught* the bus' – the direct object is the bus; 'we' are the subject.

Other examples of transitive verbs: 'You must *leave* the shop'; 'He *read* his book'.

INTRANSITIVE VERBS

These are action verbs where the action is being done, but not to anything or anyone else, e.g. 'We *ran away* quickly' – there is no direct object.

Other examples of intransitive verbs: 'It *rained*', 'He *grew up* to be a soldier'.

Some verbs can be both transitive and intransitive, e.g. you can *eat* sweets and you can *eat* every day; you *break* my heart and my *heart* breaks.

> **Insight**
> The more a verb is used in speech and writing, the more likely it is to be irregular (such as the verb 'to be').

Rarely is the question asked: is our children learning?

George W Bush

Verb tenses

The tense of a verb tells you when the action took place, either in the present, past or future. The Thai language has just one tense so the verb remains the same whether you are talking about the past, present or future. Other words in the sentence give a sense of the time in which the action is taking place (today, yesterday, right now and so on).

In English, grammarians, academics and linguistic experts argue about the number of tenses that exist. For some, there are anything up to 14 different tenses (present simple, present continuous, present perfect...). For others, there are just two set forms of verb tense: past and present ('I *rode* my bike'; 'I *ride* my bike'). Notice that there are two versions of the verb 'to ride' that indicate present and past.

In English, there is not a particular ending that indicates future tense (as other languages, like French, have). Instead, English uses additional words with the verb (such as 'will', 'will have', 'be about to' or 'shall') to show future tense ('I *will* ride my bike').

The past tense is traditionally used for story telling ('Once upon a time...'). Using the present tense gives a live, immediate feeling. Some journalists, when reporting a story that happened in the past, will use the present tense, which helps to give a sense of immediacy about their writing. Present tense can also be used for general commentary and for emphasis.

Generally, the rule is that you do not switch your tenses around when you are writing something. This is especially true if you are writing something that has a logical sequence to it (in formal writing such as a report or an essay). Mixing your tenses in the same passage of text can be confusing; are you talking about the past, present or future? For example:

▶ James walked [past tense] home and reads [present tense] the letter as he went [past tense].

Participles

A *part*iciple is a *part* of a verb and every verb has two types of participle: the present and past. You can give a strong sense of the present using the present participle '-ing' (We are *walking*, I am *reading*, they are *running*, you are *taking*).

Regular verbs can be put into the past tense by adding a past participle '-d' or '-ed' (We *walked*; she *washed*; they *floated*).

Irregular verbs, the unpredictable ones, do not follow that pattern; for example:

Present	Past
I am	I was
you go	you went
we say	we said

Insight

There are more irregular verbs in British English than there are in American. While in England, one would write 'spilt' or 'learnt' as past tense verbs; in America, it is more common to add regular past tense verb forms – 'spilled' and 'learned'.

Active and passive

When people talk about the 'voice' of a piece of writing, they are referring to either the active or passive voice. In most sentences, you have a subject, a verb and an object. In a sentence that uses the active voice (and therefore an active verb) these three elements appear in that order, subject – verb – object:

▶ The cat [subject] sat [verb] on the mat [object].
▶ The car [subject] hit [verb] the fence [object].

In these examples, 'sat' and 'hit' are the active verbs. The cat is doing the sitting, the car is doing the hitting and they both come before the object (the mat and the fence).

A sentence using the passive voice (and passive verb) reverses this order so that the object comes before the verb and is followed by the subject:

▶ The mat [object] was being sat on [verb] by the cat [subject].
▶ The fence [object] was hit [verb] by the car [subject].

The mat and the fence are the receivers of the action (sitting and hitting).

Using a form of the verb 'to be' often signals when the passive voice is being used. If you use the passive voice too much, you run the risk of repeating the same old verbs ('was', 'were') over and over again.

In most cases, the active voice is preferred to the passive. The active voice is livelier, more direct and less wordy, while the passive can be impersonal and detached:

▶ I love the children [active] = The children are loved by me [passive]

We will look at the pros and cons of using the active/passive voice in greater detail in Chapter 4.

Gerunds

Gerunds are verbs that are made to function as nouns by adding -ing.

▶ Seeing is believing.
▶ Running helps you to stay fit.
▶ Knitting can be therapeutic.
▶ We hate working at the weekend.

SUBJECTS

A verb cannot exist in a vacuum. Someone or something must also be in the sentence along with the verb performing the action – in other words, the subject.

The subject of a sentence usually (but not always) appears before the verb in a statement and after the first verb in a question:

▶ *The sun* shone brightly.
▶ Have *they* gone now?
▶ Losing *weight* takes commitment.

The subject controls whether the verb is used in its singular or plural form:

- ▶ He drinks tea.
- ▶ They drink milk.

The subject also controls other parts of a sentence:

- ▶ I dressed myself.
- ▶ She dressed herself.
- ▶ They dressed themselves.

Subjects can be:

A noun (either a single noun or a phrase):

- ▶ The bus was late.
- ▶ Kim ran away.
- ▶ Flour, milk and butter are the ingredients.

A pronoun:

- ▶ I dislike mushrooms.
- ▶ That sounds interesting.
- ▶ Who is that?

A subordinate clause:

- ▶ Where you walk is ideal.
- ▶ What we discovered was amazing.

OBJECTS

The object describes on what or on whom an action is being performed. In the sentence, 'We ate the meal', 'the meal' is the object of the verb 'eat'.

The object usually (but not always) follows the subject in a sentence. You can have direct or indirect objects.

- ▶ **Direct** – the person or thing that is directly affected by the action of the verb:
    - ▷ The dog chased the *cat*.
    - ▷ I admire *Alex*.
- ▶ **Indirect** – usually a living thing that is the recipient of the action in the sentence; a direct object is also usually present in a sentence like this and follows the indirect object:
    - ▷ He [subject] gave [verb] the child [indirect object] a present [direct object].

Objects can be:

- ▶ a noun (single noun or phrase):
  - ▷ He saw Julie.
  - ▷ We discovered a wonderful restaurant.
- ▶ a pronoun:
  - ▷ Julie saw me.
  - ▷ You said what?
- ▶ a subordinate clause:
  - ▷ He thought they were wrong.

Does grammar matter?

The art of analysing the different grammatical parts of a sentence is called 'parsing'. It is a good idea to parse what you read and write so that you can identify subjects, objects and verbs; adjectives and adverbs; prepositions and conjunctions.

The rules of grammar are not meant to restrict you or make things difficult for a writer. They are there to help us communicate clearly. Knowing the rules means you write clear, intelligible English. But grammar is only one important part of writing; the other crucial element to writing well is punctuation. When we talk, the *meaning* of what we say is helped by our body language, our tone of voice, the intonation we use, by waving our hands around or raising an eyebrow, in addition to the actual words we use. When we write, we don't have those additional aids so we use punctuation to help give meaning and tone to our words. And punctuation is what we look at in the next chapter.

10 THINGS TO TRY

1 Read through a newspaper or magazine and circle all the subjects and underline all the verbs.

2 Do the same exercise to a sample of your own writing.

3 See if you can identify all the subordinate clauses in a newspaper article, then compare this with a section from a book of fiction. Are there more or less subordinate clauses in the newspaper article?

4 Look through a sample of writing (yours, a newspaper or a report) for all words ending in -ly. If the word is an adverb, cross it out and reread the sentence. Which version works better – the one with or without the adverb?

5 Look out for weak verb/adverb combinations (e.g. 'she walked quietly') and substitute for a stronger verb (e.g. 'she crept' or 'she tiptoed'). Does it improve the sentence?

6 Underline the words that end in -ing in your writing. Are there too many? If you want to reduce them, try using a simple present or past tense and see if that strengthens your writing. Do the same for an article in a magazine or newspaper.

7 Find a passage of writing that you admire and identify all the pronouns.

8 Research some of the more unusual collective nouns.

9 Come up with a list of ten adjectives that could describe:

a) an old building   b) a baby   c) a football match.

10 Find a piece of writing that is written in the past tense; change the tense to the present. Does it make it more dramatic?

2

Punctuation

In this chapter you will learn:
- *how punctuation helps your writing*
- *how punctuation style has changed*
- *about punctuation marks and what they do*
- *when to use capital letters*.

> *Writing, when properly managed, is but a different name for conversation.*

Lawrence Sterne

When we speak, we don't actually use full stops, semicolons and commas. We may pause now and again but, in essence, as we talk a stream of words comes out. In old written texts, that is exactly what the scribes recorded – there were no breaks or spaces separating the words. The earliest punctuation marks were put there to help people who were reading out loud pause and stress the words correctly. Only in the thirteenth century did punctuation marks for printed words become more common.

If you look at a Victorian novel or essay, you will be struck at the sheer number of punctuation marks used: commas, semicolons, brackets, dashes and so on. Writers in the nineteenth century tended to write long sentences so punctuation was necessary to keep the reader on track and to guide them through to the end of the sentence. Sentences have become much shorter since the nineteenth century. Initially this was influenced by the modern punchier newspaper style and then by the internet and emails. With shorter sentences, there is less need for heavy punctuation.

But you cannot do without punctuation altogether. It does two important things: it helps reflect the sound of the 'voice' of the piece (its tone, rhythm and feeling) and it organizes the grammar so the reader understands the meaning. Used correctly, punctuation removes any ambiguity or confusion from what you are writing. In her book *Eats, Shoots and Leaves*, Lynn Truss shows how punctuation can have a major impact on the meaning of a sentence. She takes the phrase 'A woman without her man is nothing' and shows that by adding punctuation in certain ways, you can end up with two very different meanings:

▶ A woman, without her man, is nothing.
▶ A woman: without her, man is nothing.

Some writers are known for being heavy-handed with their punctuation and others prefer to use as little as possible; for example, the famous (long) soliloquy of Molly Bloom in James Joyce's *Ulysses* uses only two punctuation marks (a couple of full stops) while Tom Wolfe is not afraid to employ the exclamation mark throughout his work.

Where punctuation is concerned, it is a matter of 'style'. In this sense, you could call punctuation an art; one writer compared it to a musical score. It is how you *use* it that matters, rather than slavishly following some rules. Punctuation is there to help the reader understand what the writer intended. Used well, it can create some subtle effects.

Did you know?

Harold Ross, editor of *The New Yorker*, was fond of commas; the writer, James Thurber, was not. Ross would always add commas to Thurber's contributions to the magazine. He added one to the sentence, 'After dinner, the men went into the living room', explaining that the comma was a way of 'giving the men time to push back their chairs and stand up'.

So punctuation, even at its most basic, is fundamental to a writing style. Most people will be familiar with the full stop (period), comma and dash. Those three basic punctuation marks will get you by in English but there are several more that can raise your written communication to more sophisticated heights. Let us start with the familiar ones.

Comma (,)

Writers tend to use either too many or too few commas. The trend nowadays is to use as few as possible, as long as clarity and meaning are preserved. A sentence with two commas or less is much more direct than one that, awkwardly, if you know what I mean, has lots, and lots of commas, which, as we know, can confuse, and annoy, the reader!

It was traditional to teach that a comma should be used when you wanted to pause (take a breath) during a sentence. A comma was the short pause contrasting with the longer pause (the full stop) at the end of the sentence. While that is true, especially if you are reading the words aloud, it does not give a full description of what the comma is capable of. You can use commas for:

- ▶ **Listing** – Where you have a list of more than two things and where 'and' or 'or' could be used instead of the comma to separate items in a list: 'I saw lions, tigers, bears, giraffes and zebras' rather than 'I saw lions and tigers and...'; 'I need to buy butter, biscuits, camera, batteries'. Using the commas here helps to avoid confusion. Imagine the second sentence without the commas; is it two items, 'butter biscuits' and 'camera batteries', or four? A comma is not needed before the 'and' at the end of the list (see 'Oxford/Harvard/serial comma' later in this chapter).
- ▶ **Parentheses** – (see also 'Bracketing' later in this chapter) a pair of commas used to set off a weak interruption: 'The chicken, while strutting round the coop, let out some contented clucks'; 'We thought, on the whole, it went well.' Always remember to close the bracketing with another comma.
- ▶ **Joining** – between two clauses instead of using a conjunction like 'and', 'but', 'or', 'yet', 'while': 'Mark always got up late, yet he was rarely late for work.'
- ▶ **Consecutive adjectives** – which are equally important when it comes to describing a noun: 'A jolly, red, polka-dotted skirt.'
- ▶ **Omission** – used to show that words have been left out instead of repeated: 'It was a noisy, dirty train' – rather than write 'noisy and dirty' the comma takes the place of 'and'.
- ▶ **Before direct speech** – e.g. He said, 'I don't know.' Although this use seems to be dropping out of fashion (see 'Quotation Marks' later in this chapter).

- ▶ **Introductory words** – such as 'for example', 'for instance' (although this style is also changing and commas are being used less and less here).
- ▶ **Setting apart a name from the rest of the sentence** – e.g. 'More tea, Vicar?' 'Mary, let's get going.'
- ▶ **Setting apart an exclamation or interjection** – e.g. 'Goodness, that was a surprise!'
- ▶ **Numbers of four digits or more** – e.g. 3,150. Use a comma after every third digit, reading from right to left.

WHEN NOT TO USE A COMMA

- ▶ If you want to join two complete sentences, e.g. 'Jane loves bread, Ann dislikes cheese', because the comma is not strong enough to hold the two together on its own. This is called a 'comma splice' and is grammatically incorrect. Use either a semicolon or rewrite the sentence: 'Jane loves bread; Ann dislikes cheese' or 'Jane loves bread while Ann dislikes cheese.'
- ▶ With compound words: i.e. 'a beautiful Christmas tree' has no comma between 'beautiful' and 'Christmas' because we are referring to a 'Christmas tree' (a compound word) rather than a tree that is beautiful and Christmas. A compound word is one that is formed by two words joined together to make a new word (e.g. 'sand' and 'paper' have two distinct meanings; put together they form a compound word, 'sand paper'; other examples: 'French poodle', 'Scotch egg, 'China tea).
- ▶ After a number: 'Two, cats; three, apples' is incorrect. 'Two cats; three apples' is correct.
- ▶ To separate words that indicate a number or amount, such as 'more', 'less', etc.: 'many cats', 'few apples'.
- ▶ After the abbreviations 'i.e.' and 'e.g.': commas – and full stops – used to be standard, but these abbreviations have become so common that they are no longer needed.

Insight

To check whether you need a comma or not between several adjectives, try inserting 'and' where you plan to put the commas. If it sounds odd, you probably don't need commas (e.g. 'six antique lacquered red chairs' – no commas are needed because you would never write 'six and antique and lacquered and red chairs'; 'sad *and* misunderstood' – you can use a comma here: 'sad, misunderstood').

This kind of comma goes before the final 'and' or 'nor' in a sentence:

▶ The bag held his clothes, shoes, and books.

British English tends not use the serial comma, while standard usage in American English is to leave it in. You rarely see it in newspapers mainly because they are keen to save space where they can. This style of comma is becoming outdated so you will see it less and less.

Generally, a sentence makes sense whether you have a serial comma or not:

▶ 'I love waving a red, white, and blue flag' has the same meaning as 'I love waving a red, white and blue flag'.

There *are* occasions when it is useful because it makes the sentence clearer. For example:

▶ 'I sat with George, my doctor and my friend' – one person
▶ 'I sat with George, my doctor, and my friend' – three people.

Use it:

▶ if the items in the list are rather long: 'We visited the tomb of Shakespeare, the dungeons of Warwick Castle, and all the stately homes in the area'
▶ if an item in the list already contains the word 'and': 'We ordered ham and eggs, chicken and chips, and wine' – the comma after 'chips' tells you that 'chicken and chips' are an item.

Full stop/period (.)

This is probably the most straightforward of all punctuation marks to understand and use. A full stop comes at the end of a sentence. It is difficult to overuse the full stop (or 'period' in American English). In its style guide to journalists, *The Times* says that the best punctuation is the full stop and advises its journalists to avoid showing off with 'dashes'.

▶ The rule has been that you use a full stop with an abbreviation, such as no. (number), co. (company), Rev. (Reverend) and Prof. (Professor) but this is another 'rule' that seems to be falling out of fashion. So you don't have to use a full stop with an abbreviation but it can be useful if you want to avoid any confusion (for example: 'no' could mean the word 'no' or the abbreviation for 'number'. A full stop afterwards shows that it is an abbreviation.).

▶ You don't need to use a full stop at the end of abbreviations that have been contracted, such as Mrs – mistress, Dr – doctor, St – saint. You can tell it's a contraction if the last letter is the same as in the full word.

The full stop has an internet alter-ego, called 'dot', which is an important part of internet and email addresses. Be careful about ending a sentence with an email address or URL. If you add a full stop as punctuation (rather than a dot as part of the address), you can confuse your reader who may not be sure if the full stop is actually a dot, part of the address, or a full stop.

Insight

Always use punctuation at the end of sentences: a full stop (or period), exclamation or question mark. Don't put more than one mark at the end of your sentence unless you are happy to look like an idiot!!!!?!!!!

If you are one of those people who learned to type on a typewriter, you will have been taught to leave two spaces after a full stop. The space bar on a typewriter leaves the same space whether it is between words or at the end of a sentence. So to make a strong visual break at the end of a sentence, two spaces were needed. That is no longer necessary if you use a computer. Computer software recognizes the end of sentences. If you find the two-space habit hard to break, you can continue to leave two spaces but be aware that this can leave odd-looking blocks of space.

Dash (–)

The dash has a slightly more informal air than other punctuation marks – using it makes the tone more conversational and colloquial.

Use a dash if you want to interrupt the flow of a sentence and add some information in the middle of it. You can do that in the middle of the sentence – so you will need a pair of dashes – before carrying on to the end of the sentence. You can also use it to add a clause at the end of the sentence – in which case you only need one dash.

Dashes are useful:

- ▶ to break the continuity of a sentence: 'I don't believe it – they've arrived already.'
- ▶ to add emphasis or repetition: 'It's cheese, Jo – cheese – not poison.'
- ▶ for broken sentences: 'Do – you – understand – what – I – am – saying?'
- ▶ instead of commas or brackets: 'We will carry on – never stopping – until we reach the end.'
- ▶ to show something is incomplete: 'Well, I'll be –'
- ▶ to show a range of something: 1567–1667; pages 12–34.

Insight

Keep your use of dashes to a minimum; they are not easy to read and text can look chopped up and bitty if there are too many dashes scattered around. *Never* use more than one pair of dashes in a sentence

Semicolon (;)

George Orwell did not like them; Charles Dickens did. Abraham Lincoln called it 'a useful little chap'; George Bernard Shaw complained that T. E. Lawrence didn't use enough of them. Personal style and preference seem to guide the use of the semicolon, although they are becoming less popular (to be replaced with a dash in many cases). Even newspapers are abandoning them, preferring shorter sentences and brief paragraphs so they are rarely needed.

A semicolon marks a stronger break than a comma but not quite as definite as a full stop. When a reader comes across a semicolon, they pause but not for long. The semicolon tells you that more information is coming, something that is *related* to the clause you have just read. They are useful to link slightly shorter sentences together so you have a more flowing text, rather than a lot of choppy little sentences.

Semicolons can take the place of co-ordinating conjunctions (and, but, or, nor, for, yet) to link two closely linked or related sentences:

- ▶ I'd love to go abroad on holiday this year; it's just difficult with my job situation.
- ▶ She was born in Birmingham; she moved to Bournemouth in her teens.

If you are listing things that include commas in the individual items of the list, separate these items with a semicolon, for example:

The menu was great. It included steak and kidney pie, chips and peas; roast beef, Yorkshire pudding and seasonal vegetables; a pasta dish, with salad, an Italian dressing and garlic bread; apple pie, ice cream; cheese and biscuits.

Don't use semicolons:

▶ to join nouns together, unless you are listing them: 'The suitcase contained all we needed such as clothes; shoes; toiletries; books; camera; sun hats' – commas would be more appropriate here.

▶ to join two unrelated clauses together: 'She loved walking the dog; her favourite flowers are daffodils' – have as two separate sentences.

Colon (:)

A colon comes after a complete sentence and indicates to the reader that there is something to follow that will expand on, explain or amplify the meaning in the first complete sentence:

▶ We only had three counties left to visit: Devon, Cornwall and Somerset.

You don't need to put a capital letter after the colon unless, as in the above example, you are using a proper noun. Don't use a colon after a sentence fragment.

They are also used:

▶ to formally introduce lists, 'as in this example: use the colon to go before the first item in the list, follow it with a comma, and then finish with a full stop.'
▶ at the beginning of a long quotation
▶ when a book, film or sub-title follows a main title (*The Writer's Guide to Good Style: A practical guide for twenty-first century writers*).

Insight

If you are not sure whether you can use a colon or not, try substituting the word 'namely' where you want to put the colon. If it fits and makes sense, then you can insert a colon ('Our tour takes in several European cities, namely Paris, Rome, Zurich').

Don't feel you have to use a colon just because you are about to list something. The colon is useful if you have to jump straight into a list without much preamble or introduction.

Parentheses (() [] „ – – {})

One writer described them as bookends for short statements. The words inside the parentheses tend to act as a sort of aside; they add clarity or extra information to what is being said but they are not a major part of the main sentence:

▶ You can read about pruning roses (pages 12–14) and shrubs (pages 26–8).

Parentheses can be:

▶ brackets (like this) or [like this]
▶ dashes – such as these –
▶ commas, like this,
▶ curly or brace brackets {used in mathematics, poetry and music}.

Technically, the words inside the parentheses should have no grammatical effect on what is outside. If you use commas in a parenthetical way, the words inside the commas are still part of the sentence, though, and should be treated as such.

Square brackets [such as these] are used when you are quoting and need to add some words of your own so that the reader knows that you have added something that was not part of the original quote, either to clarify or to make an editorial comment. For example, the original quote might have been:

▶ We went down to the docks and boarded it.

That sentence makes perfect sense in the context of the whole speech but, as you are taking that sentence out of context, you need to clarify what is being said. Therefore, it makes sense to write:

▶ We went down to the docks and boarded [the ship].

Square brackets are also used to surround the word 'sic' (Latin for 'thus, so') which shows that any error or oddity such as a spelling mistake or something that looks like a mistake but isn't one was made by the original speaker/writer and not the current writer. You can sometimes also use square brackets with an ellipsis to show when words have been left out [...].

Ordinary brackets tend to be used when the writer is adding extra information; where dashes can interrupt a sentence rather abruptly:

▶ The FDR (Flight Data Recorder) was recovered from the ocean.

If a parenthetical comment is part of a larger sentence, put the full stop after the second bracket (like this). (In some cases, you may have to use a whole sentence enclosed in brackets; in which case, put the full stop inside the second bracket.)

Apostrophe (')

The apostrophe has two uses. It shows contraction and possession.

CONTRACTION

Use an apostrophe to show that a letter or letters are missing (I *can't* see why *you're* cross = I *cannot* see why *you are* cross). Be careful with some words that sound the same but, if they have an apostrophe, can mean something quite different:

▶ You're [contraction] in trouble with your [possession] mother = you are in trouble with your mother.

Particular mention should go to 'it's' here. When 'it's' has an apostrophe, it is indicating that the writer means 'it is' or 'it has': It's been raining all day; it's very wet outside.' 'Its' – without an apostrophe – shows possession: 'The dog wagged *its* tail.'

POSSESSION

There are two ways to show possession in English. The longer, more wordy version is similar to the way the French language works:

▶ the pen of my aunt, the hat of the boy, the mission statement of the company.

Or you can use the apostrophe:

▶ my aunt's pen, the boy's hat, the company's mission statement.

To show ownership of a single noun, add apostrophe 's': the dog's dinner (the dinner of one dog). Most plurals already end in 's' in

English so to indicate possession of a plural noun, add the apostrophe after the 's': the dogs' dinner (the dinner of several dogs).

For those special words that act as plural nouns (mice, teeth, men, children), add apostrophe 's': the men's cars. We look at plurals and apostrophes in more detail in Chapter 5.

In addition, use the apostrophe to:

▶ indicate quantity or time – 'take three pound's worth', 'give two week's notice'
▶ show when letters have been left out – 'Give 'im it, we'd've gone sooner'. Also used in poetry a lot; e.g. 'o'er' (over), 'n'er' (never), 't'was' (it was) and 'ta'en' (taken)
▶ write Irish names, such as O'Casey, O'Grady
▶ show plurals of letters (mind your p's and q's)
▶ show plurals of words (and's, if's and but's).

When not to use an apostrophe

Never use an apostrophe to denote a plural. For example, the following are all wrong:

▶ Apple's and pear's for sale (apples and pears – correct)
▶ 100's of CD's for sale (100s of CDs – correct)
▶ MOT's for car's and van's (MOTs for cars and vans – correct)

The apostrophe and abbreviations: newspapers and magazines used to write about CD's, MP's and LP's but the trend now, certainly in Britain, is to drop the apostrophe altogether (CDs, MPs) – unless you are talking about a possessive (the CD's case, the MP's expenses). Again, it looks cleaner and neater. You do not need an apostrophe when talking about decades or ages (the *1960s* were all about free love; people in their *60s* are still very active).

The disappearing apostrophe is a trend that has continued with road signs, notices and shop names since designers are aiming for a less fussy, more modern look. Various councils in England have taken the decision to ban the use of apostrophes on street signs – to the dismay of many. There are a few place names that retain the apostrophe, such as Martha's Vineyard, King's Lynn, Bishop's Castle.

Hyphen (-)

I think the most un-American thing in the world is a hyphen.

Woodrow Wilson

A hyphen is a short horizontal line, like a dash, but shorter. The main use of a hyphen is to join words together (a dash keeps them apart); this kind of word is called a 'compound word' (such as flower-pot, self-service, anti-aircraft).

You will find a huge inconsistency in the way compound words are combined. Some are written as single words, as hyphenated words and as two words, e.g. 'cry baby', 'cry-baby', 'crybaby'. In 2007, the sixth edition of the *Shorter Oxford English Dictionary* got rid of around 16,000 hyphenated words, turning them into either two separate words ('ice cream', instead of 'ice-cream') or one word ('bumble-bee' became 'bumblebee'). The editor, Angus Stephenson, explained that the decision was made because people were not confident about using hyphens anymore and they made print look messy and old-fashioned so were generally being dropped from adverts and websites anyway. Many words that we use nowadays (such as lifelike, bedroom, wheelbarrow, seaside, girlfriend, today) began life with a hyphen in the middle of them.

If you are still keen to use hyphens when describing something but still not sure where they should go, remember:

▶ If the description comes after the noun, don't use a hyphen ('my dog is long haired'; 'the beef was well done').
▶ If the description comes before the noun, use a hyphen ('a long-haired dog', 'well-done beef)' because without a hyphen, the phrase could be somewhat ambiguous ('long haired dog': is it a long dog with hair or a dog with long hair?).

- If both descriptive words can stand alone and be used separately, don't use a hyphen (well-done needs a hyphen because you wouldn't have 'done beef' and 'well beef'; however, with 'small blue hat' both 'small' and 'blue' can stand alone and describe the hat so there is no need for a hyphen).
- If you are using self-, quasi-, pro- or ex-, you will always need a hyphen (self-obsessed, quasi-academic, ex-boxer).
- You will need a hyphen if you are repeating or duplicating certain words ('hush-hush').
- Use a hyphen if you add a beginning or ending to a word that starts with a capital letter: anti-American, Yuppie-like.
- Use a hyphen when linking a noun with a noun (Simplon-Orient-Express).
- You should not need to use a hyphen after 'very' ('a very large mouse'), 'most', 'least' or 'less'.
- Always use a hyphen if the beginning or ending would create a double vowel or a double or triple consonant (shell-like, de-ice, co-wrote, co-ordinate, co-op), although many publishers' style sheets indicate a preference for 'cooperate', 'coordinate' and so on.
- Use hyphens when writing out numbers between 21 and 99 in full (twenty-one, ninety-nine).
- When you spell out a word and you want to picture the letters separately, use hyphens to separate each letter *('That's Keynsham: K-E-Y-N-S-H-A-M')*.
- If you have to split a word over two lines and you want to show that the word is not finished, use a hyphen. This is less of a problem with modern computers because they shunt a word onto a new line automatically. If you do find you have to split a word, be careful where the split occurs so that you don't end up with an odd looking half (e.g. 'out-standing' is better than 'outs-tanding') or an unfortunate misunderstanding ('the-rapist' instead of 'therapist').

The hyphen is extremely useful at avoiding confusion or to give correct pronunciation to a word that might otherwise give a different meaning:

- 'I need to re-press my shirt' makes more sense than 'I need to repress my shirt.
- 'Six year-old dogs' (year old dogs multiplied by six) is a very different description from 'six-year-old dogs' (dogs that are six years old).

▶ A 'great-grandfather' is not necessarily the same as a 'great grandfather'.

Certainly, American English seems reluctant to use the hyphen with words that begin with re-. Yet there can be a significant difference if you add a hyphen or leave one out. For example:

resort	re-sort
reform	re-form
recollect	re-collect
recede	re-cede
remark	re-mark

Use a hyphen if you think there is any chance of misleading your reader.

Exclamation mark (!)

Also known informally as a 'bang', this is a straightforward punctuation mark that indicates surprise, urgency, panic or fear; any strong emotion really (What!). It can also indicate loudness of voice.

There is a tendency for some writers to overuse it enthusiastically! Crime writer, Elmore Leonard, believes two or three exclamation marks every 100,000 words is more than enough. It should be used sparingly and always at the end of a sentence. It is rarely seen in newspapers and should not appear in formal business writing. And you do not need to add one every time you want to emphasize a point or fact. Aaaagh!!!!!

Did you know?
Chekov wrote a short story, *The Exclamation Mark*, about a civil servant who realizes with horror that he has never used an exclamation mark in an official document.

Question mark (?)

This only ever finishes off a sentence so it is a kind of extremely specialized full stop. Use when asking a direct question:

▶ Have you cleaned the fish out today?

But *not* after an indirect or implied question in reported speech:

▶ He wondered if she had cleaned the fish out.

Implied questions tend to have phrases such as 'I wonder' and 'Guess what' in them. If you use a direct question as an order ('Can the workforce arrive an hour earlier next Monday?'), the use of the questions mark is technically correct but some people choose to leave it out which is fine. Using the question mark in this case makes it more of a request; leaving the question mark out makes it an order. The choice of tone is up to you.

Did you know?
Printer Henry Denham introduced a back-to-front question mark in the sixteenth century to indicate a rhetorical question but the idea never caught on.

Quotation marks (' ' " ")

Also known as 'inverted commas', 'speech marks', or the more casual 'quotes', you use quotation marks when you are writing a conversation (called 'direct speech') or you are reporting someone's exact words. Whatever is inside the quotation marks is assumed to be exactly what was said (if you are quoting another person). If you make any changes to that quote – for example, you may wish to shorten it by leaving a few words out – you have to indicate this with either ellipsis, brackets or the word 'sic' (see 'Parentheses' earlier in this chapter).

You need to know who is speaking so what is said is usually accompanied by a reporting clause. This clause can come before, during or after what is being said:

▶ Colin shouted, 'You won't catch me because I'm too fast.'
▶ 'You won't catch me because I'm too fast,' Colin shouted.
▶ 'You won't catch me,' shouted Colin, 'because I'm too fast.'

You usually put a comma before the opening quote of who is about to speak:

▶ Steve said, 'I don't feel well!'

However, some writers are dropping this comma and using either a colon to introduce the direct speech (Steve said: 'I don't feel well!') or no punctuation mark at all. It is up to you which one you favour but it does seem worth having something before the quotation marks, unless the speech is very short, to indicate to the reader that direct speech is coming.

If you are writing dialogue, you may need to interrupt someone's speech. For example,

▶ 'It was such a good idea,' Beatrice remarked, 'to avoid the motorway.'

The original speech stays the same; there is no capital letter starting off the second part of the quote because it is all one original sentence. If the second quote was a new sentence, you would need a capital letter to start it, and a full stop, rather than a comma, before it:

▶ 'It was such a good idea to avoid the motorway,' Beatrice remarked. 'We should avoid the traffic.'

You need the quotation marks, though, to know who is speaking and what they are saying. Note that you have two commas when interrupting speech: one at the end of the first part of the speech (inside the quotation marks) and the second just before the second half of the speech starts, after the person who is speaking and before the quotation marks start.

As you know, there are single and double quotation marks on a keyboard. In print, standard British use is leaning towards using the single mark; it looks less fussy. If you then quote within the quotation, you use the double marks, for example:

▶ 'I didn't understand what was happening when he shouted "Get down!" at me.'

American style uses double quotation marks (plus single if quoting within a quote as above); whichever style you choose, make sure you are consistent throughout your writing.

Writing a quotation as a sentence or two can be put within a paragraph. If you are writing about a more detailed, lengthier conversation (perhaps in fiction) or quoting a conversation, you must start a new line/paragraph every time the *speaker* changes; you don't need to start a new line for every new speech. This makes things much easier to follow and your reader is not left wondering who said what to whom. If a speech runs to more than one paragraph, start it off with a quotation mark but don't finish the first (or following) paragraphs with a quotation mark; only the opening paragraphs of the same speech have quotation marks. When the speech is finished, and only then, do you close it off with a quotation mark.

If you are using a short quotation, about three lines, put it in quotation marks within the text. If you are using a longer piece that would make a paragraph in its own right, you don't need quotation marks. Indent the start of the quote, on a new line with a line space before and after it so it stands out from the rest of the text.

Insight

If you have to make loads of changes to a quotation, it is probably a better idea to paraphrase what someone has said, in which case you do not need to use quotation marks.

Quotation marks can be used to show sarcasm or irony around certain words. These are also known as 'scare' quotes.

▶ Dad's lying down; he's feeling a bit 'fragile'. (i.e. Dad's got a hangover).

QUOTATION MARKS – BRITISH AND AMERICAN PUNCTUATION

British and American English sometimes differ over where to put the punctuation in and around quotation marks. American English always puts the commas and full stops/periods inside the quotation marks; British English punctuation is outside (although the American form seems to be gaining ground in Britain) unless it is direct speech where the end punctuation belongs inside the quotation marks.

▶ Direct speech, UK and US – Sam said, 'I am not sure.'
▶ UK – They all agreed she was a true 'pillar of society'.
▶ US – They all agreed she was a true "pillar of society."

If the actual quotation is an exclamation or question, put the relevant punctuation inside the quote marks regardless of country. If, however, the whole statement, which includes the quotation, is an exclamation/ question then the punctuation will go at the end of the whole sentence:

▶ 'What can Mary have meant when she said, "I don't like bus travel"?'

Writing (or saying) 'quotation marks' is quite a mouthful every time. Informally, people refer to 'quote marks' although that is strictly not accurate. A 'quote' is what you do and a quotation is the text that you are quoting but it is acceptable to use the more informal version.

> **Punctuation to the writer is like anatomy to the artist: He learns the rules so he can knowledgeably and, with control, depart from them as art requires. Punctuation is a means, and its end is: helping the reader to hear, to follow.**
>
> Thomas McCormack, *The Fiction Editor, the Novel and the Novelist*

Ellipsis (...)

In Greek, an ellipsis (plural 'ellipses') means 'an omission'. An ellipsis is the omission of words from a sentence or phrase. Words can be left out to avoid repetition or shorten the sentence. For example, most people would write the following:

▶ Jane has been to Spain but Norman hasn't.

Rather than:

▶ Jane has been to Spain but Norman hasn't been to Spain.

The repetition would be unnecessary and bore the reader so it makes sense to leave it out; this is an ellipsis. If you are going to leave words out, make sure that the meaning of the clause still remains so you do not confuse the reader.

In the above example, there is no indication of the ellipsis; it is understood. You can show an ellipsis using the correct punctuation mark (also called an ellipsis): three evenly spaced dots (or periods/full stops) with or without spaces on either side (depending on preferred style) that shows when words or phrases have been intentionally left out of a sentence. Many fonts have a symbol for the ellipsis but it is perfectly acceptable to type three full stops or periods; just make sure they do not run over onto a second line.

An ellipsis is useful if you want to keep your quotation shorter or avoid repetition:

▶ The presentation was arranged to honour the ten heads of state from the various European countries who were visiting the UN.
▶ The presentation was arranged to honour the ten heads of state... who were visiting the UN.

Remember, the ellipsis is standing in for a missing word/s so make sure there is a space either side of it (although the preferred style of some publishing houses, including this one, is to omit these spaces). If you are using ellipsis to paraphrase a statement, you must be careful to preserve the meaning of the sentence. Removing words can, if not done carefully, change the original meaning.

In American English, if the omission comes at the end of a sentence, you use the full stop and then the three dots – making four 'dots' in total. In this instance, there is a space between the three dots of the ellipsis and the full stop. In British English, an ellipsis is only ever three dots, though may be followed by an exclamation mark or question mark.

You can use an ellipsis to show a pause in the flow of a sentence or a tailing off into silence:

▶ We argued and cogitated...and then cogitated and argued a bit more.
▶ John, look out! He's got a gun. He's going to...

Interrobang (‽)

The interrobang is a non-standard punctuation mark that you may come across. It combines a question mark with an exclamation mark. It was invented in the early 1960s and was intended to be used to indicate asking a question in either an excited or disbelieving manner. The actual symbol or glyph is not standard on many PCs (you can find an interrobang as a special character in Wingdings 2 and Palatino) and so it's regarded as something of a passing fashion...but it hasn't quite died away.

Writers can get the same effect by using multiple punctuation marks, usually a question mark followed by an exclamation mark. It is not something you would want to see in formal writing but it does appear in blogs and other informal types of communication.

Slash/solidus/virgule (/)

This is not the prettiest of punctuation marks and should be used lightly. It is a short slash between two words where the reader can choose the most appropriate word, such as 'and/or'.

- ▶ It can indicate a period of time (1965/66).
- ▶ You can also use it to separate lines of verse when it is not possible to present the words in the original layout ('I wandered lonely as a cloud / That floats on high o'er vales and hills, / When all at once I saw a crowd, / A host, of golden daffodils').
- ▶ It can be used to show an abbreviation (c/o = care of; a/c = account).
- ▶ It is used in URLs (website addresses) and computer programs.

Asterisk (*)

Asterisks are useful if you need to replace letters in an offensive word ('It was a b****y long way'). They are also used at the end of a word, phrase, sentence or paragraph to indicate that there is an explanation or footnote elsewhere in the text.

Capital letters

Capital letters guide the eye through the sentences and paragraphs of text. They act like signposts. Capital letters should be used:

- ▶ at the start of sentences, direct quotations and direct questions
- ▶ at the start of titles, headings and sub-headings
- ▶ for all proper nouns which include:
    - ▷ people's names
    - ▷ organization and company names
    - ▷ place names (streets, towns, counties, states, countries)
    - ▷ particular days (Mother's Day, Valentine's Day, Christmas Day)
    - ▷ days and months (Monday, April)
    - ▷ religions (and religious holidays) (Methodism, Easter)
    - ▷ languages and nationalities (Italian, Dutch, Asian, African) because the names are taken from the name of the country
    - ▷ geographical areas (the Deep South, the North East, the West End) when referring to a specific parts of a country or area, although this varies and often caps are not used, e.g. the north-east of England or south-west London.
- ▶ abbreviated titles (such as Mr, Mrs, Dr, Rev.)
- ▶ adjectives that are taken from proper nouns (the American people, an Orwellian nightmare)

- abbreviations (BBC, USA, PC) – you do not need to put full stops after the letters
- some acronyms – words made from the initial letters of other words (NASA, OPEC); you do not need to put full stops after the letters
- when referring to a specific organization or titled person, for example: 'The Government is reviewing its policy on immigration' is referring to a specific government; 'The Prime Minister met other heads of state' refers to the particular holder of the title
- words that refer to God. Traditionally, those that believed in a deity tended to capitalize whatever name they used, including referring to 'He' and 'Him'. Nowadays, even some churches have given up capitalizing the name of god but if you are unsure, use the capital to avoid giving offence. The names of mythological gods only have a capital if you refer to them by their name (Zeus, Apollo, etc.).

You do not need to use capitals:

- for the first letter of every word in a document heading or in subheadings
- for some acronyms – some have become so well known (radar, laser) that they no longer need a capital letter at the beginning
- when referring to an organization in general: e.g. 'Local councils are unhappy with the policy development' is describing a number of councils, rather than any specific one
- if you are talking about direction: 'We flew south' rather than 'We flew South'
- for seasons (winter, summer, spring, autumn) or times of the day (noon, midnight)
- FOR WRITING WHOLE PHRASES OR SENTENCES.

It is hard to start a sentence without a capital letter if you use a computer; the word processing package will not allow you to use a lower case letter.

Did you know?

Capital letters are also known as 'upper case'; 'lower case' is for all the other letters. The name comes from traditional printing where the individual letters were kept in boxes. Capital letters were kept in the upper cases and the rest were in the lower cases.

The case for using good punctuation

Punctuation adds tone, meaning and sense to what we write. Without it, we would struggle to make sense of what is written. There are some hard and fast punctuation rules but, for the most part, how one uses it is up to the individual writer.

The trend nowadays is towards shorter sentences and paragraphs so there is less need to break up long and complicated phrases to aid understanding. However, that does not mean that we can get by with minimal punctuation. We should aim for a balance that makes the meaning clear but does not clutter up the page with lots of punctuation marks.

The look of the page – how we present what we write – is what we will cover in the next chapter.

10 THINGS TO TRY

1 Write something (it can be anything) but leave out all the punctuation marks. Get a friend to read the passage back to you out loud.

2 Copy a passage of text from a newspaper but remove all the capital letters. See whether it is easier or more difficult to read with or without the capital letters.

3 Look at a novel by Charles Dickens or Jane Austen. Compare their use of punctuation to a popular writer today.

4 Compare the punctuation in a tabloid newspaper with that of an official document or formal report. Do they use the same punctuation marks? More or fewer?

5 Practise using semicolons. Replace co-ordinating conjunctions with a semicolon and see whether it affects the flow of the text.

6 Look out for brackets/parentheses as you read. Try substituting these () for other brackets, commas and/or dashes. Does this change the meaning or not?

7 Keep looking for apostrophes and how they are used. Can you find any examples of incorrect use?

8 If you see multiple use of exclamation marks (more than one at a time), mentally remove all but one. Does this change the meaning? Is the impact lessened or intensified?

9 Practise using ellipses. Take long sentences from a newspaper article and try to shorten them, using an ellipsis, without losing the sense of the sentence.

10 Study how writers handle quotation marks: in a factual piece (newspaper or magazine) and in a work of fiction.

3

....

Appearance and presentation

In this chapter you will learn:
- *the structure of sentences*
- *the importance of layout and design*
- *how to use titles and headings*
- *about using visuals to make the text stand out.*

> *Writing is risk-taking. We bungee jump from a sentence and pray the cord stops short of catastrophe.*
>
> Arthur Plotnik

Chapters 1 and 2 looked at grammar and punctuation – the basic tools you need to write clearly and effectively. But writing is more than getting the semicolon in the right place and not mixing up your tenses. Vague phrases, poor sentence structure and a complicated page layout all contribute to confusing our readers. How you present your writing – what it looks like – is just as important.

In this chapter, we will go back to the basic structure of writing (word order, sentences, paragraphs and so on) and look at the tools we can use as writers to present our words to the greatest effect.

Word order

The sequence of words matters in English if you want your sentences to make sense. In Latin, you don't have this problem because the ending of the words tell you which one is the subject and which the object; in theory, you could scatter the Latin words any which way in a sentence and they would still make sense.

Generally, in English, your order would be: subject – verb – object. This is the most common word order used and it gives clear meaning to most sentences. There are obviously lots of ways to play around with that order and, in fiction, poetry and other descriptive forms, writers will do just that. If you invert the order in other types of writing (a report, for example) you run the risk of drawing attention away from what you are saying and onto the format you are using.

Sentences

I got into my bones the essential structure of the ordinary British sentence – which is a noble thing.

Winston Churchill

H.W. Fowler, George Orwell and almost every other commentator on the use of the English language say that a writer should be brief. The dictionary definition of brevity is the 'concise and exact use of words in writing or speech'. So it doesn't mean using as few words as possible or dropping every other word in a sentence in order to keep it short. It *does* mean trimming the fat off your sentences, keeping to the point and making the words work hard so that you get your meaning across without lapsing into verbal diarrhoea. We would all prefer to read 200 words rather than 500.

You can be brief and concise if you structure your sentences carefully. If you are unsure what you are trying to say, you can let your sentences run on and on without coming to any satisfactory conclusion. Sentences have been shrinking over the years. The average Elizabethan sentence was about 45 words long; the Victorians used 29 on average. Nowadays, we favour a much shorter sentence (about 20 words or less). Writers want to catch their reader's attention quickly and hold it. It is easier to do that with short, easily understood sentences that can be read quickly.

Sentences come in all shapes and sizes. They can contain one word or many, one statement or several; they allow us to ask questions, make statements, demand action and express emotions. A sentence is a group of words that makes complete sense. 'I fed the fish' is a complete correctly constructed sentence; 'I fed' is not. A sentence should contain at least one clause.

Remember, a clause = subject + verb.

The purpose of a sentence is to move the sense or message of whatever you are writing one step further on. Each sentence is part of that chain of understanding, so they need to work together. A good sentence allows a reader to digest the information quickly and move on to the next one.

There are four different types of sentence:

- ▶ **declarative** – make an assertion or statement: 'The wood is next to the house'
- ▶ **interrogative** – ask a question: 'Where did I leave my bag?'
- ▶ **imperative** – gives a command or direction: 'See if the mail has arrived'; 'Please send it to me'
- ▶ **exclamatory** – expressing emotion: 'I'll cry.'

COMPLETE SENTENCES

Complete sentences are straightforward sentences which can be divided up into:

- ▶ **simple** – single clause: 'I went shopping yesterday'
- ▶ **compound** – two or more clauses: 'I went shopping yesterday but didn't find anything to buy'
- ▶ **complex** – at least one main clause + subordinate clause: 'I went shopping yesterday, despite the weather, but didn't find anything to buy.'

The length of a sentence is often dictated by how formal or informal the writing is. If you are texting or emailing a friend, you will probably use much shorter sentence fragments (see later); while a report or formal letter will have complete sentences.

INCOMPLETE (FRAGMENT) SENTENCES

A 'normal' sentence is usually made up of subject – verb – object and has, in essence, a beginning, middle and end. But you can also use incomplete sentences. A fragment. Like that one. As long it makes sense to the reader. We use them all the time in speech. They are ideal for short expressions ('What?'), catchphrases ('An eye for an eye') and greetings ('Hi!'). Short cuts are the norm with text messaging and emails so people are quite comfortable with truncated sentences but they do have to be intelligible.

- ▶ They help add a different rhythm to a piece of writing.
- ▶ You can avoid messy repetition if you use them.

Modern writing has a much more conversational style which is suited to sentence fragments. But there is no substitute for longer sentences, which give a fuller tone and voice quality. If you haven't given enough information, it can be hard for the reader to interpret your message. A combination of long and short sentences can be more effective than using one or the other.

LENGTH OF SENTENCE

Controlled sentences deliver precise language in an emphatic arrangement based on logic, economy and clarity, all to engage the reader.

Spunk & Bite, Arthur Plotnik (Random House, 2005)

Some of the earliest books were bibles. They were read out loud in churches and monasteries. 'Silent reading' was almost unheard of. In the fourth century, the discovery of Ambrose, the Bishop of Milan, reading to himself was considered remarkable. Even though silent reading is the norm nowadays, our inner ear is tuned to the rhythm of the words on a page. If something sounds good to that inner ear, it is easier to read and understand. If the rhythm becomes predictable, the reader gets bored.

Sentence length directly affects the rhythm. It is difficult to prescribe the 'right' number of words to have in a sentence. If we said that having 20 words per sentence was an ideal length that does not mean that you should have every sentence at 20 words. The danger of writing to such a strict formula is that it becomes monotonous to read, not to mention extremely difficult to write. You need variety to create rhythm and to keep the reader interested.

Be careful with long sentences as well. The longer a sentence is, the greater the concentration needed to take it all in, understand it and get to the end without having to return to the beginning to wonder what it was all about in the end. That sentence was 45 words long, by the way. If you are confident that you have the attention of your reader, then you can get away with the odd long sentence. But it does not necessarily show that you are a good writer. If it makes the reader go back and re-read it because they didn't understand it the first time of reading, it is not a good sentence.

Long-winded sentences are usually the result of trying to cram in too many ideas and thoughts. Anything over three statements in a sentence runs the risk of being confusing or too complex. It takes a very good writer to steer the reader through multiple ideas and punctuation within one sentence. It is easier for both writer and reader to keep sentences shorter but of a variable length.

Insight

Vary your sentence length to mix up the rhythm. That keeps your readers interested, engaged and comprehending what is being said. You are in control of the pace for your reader. It is up to you to slow things down and speed things up.

Did you know?

There are some extremely restrictive forms of creative writing. A Shakespearean sonnet has fourteen lines, with ten syllables on each line and uses iambic pentameter (an unstressed syllable, followed by a stressed syllable, repeated five times). A haiku is a Japanese poem which has three lines and is made up of 17 syllables in total (five on the first line; seven on the second, five on the last line).

O fan of white silk,
Clear as frost on the grass-blade.
You are also laid aside.

Ezra Pound

Paragraphs

According to Simon Heffer in his book *Strictly English* (Random House, 2010), the definition of a paragraph is: 'a distinct passage or section of text, usually composed of several sentences, dealing with a particular point, a short episode in a narrative, a single piece of direct speech, etc.'

Paragraphs, like sentences, have become shorter. Victorian writers would only start a new paragraph when their train of thought or argument changed. Nowadays, the subject matter of several paragraphs may stay the same, each one representing part of an idea or theme.

The contents of a paragraph will differ from writer to writer. A complicated, involved argument may be put into one paragraph by one writer but divided up into several shorter ones by another. However long or short your paragraphs are, they should contain one clear topic that is relevant to the greater whole.

▶ Short paragraphs are easy to understand and can be scanned quickly.
▶ They are popular with newspapers, which need to convey stories in easily read sections.
▶ Some of the tabloid newspapers only have a couple of sentences to a paragraph.
▶ Even with short paragraphs, get your main points in at the beginning of the paragraph; don't pad the start with waffle and then get round to your point.

Leave a line space between paragraphs. This breaks up the text, gives a bit of white space and makes it easier for the reader to take in. If space is at a premium, you can omit the extra line space and indent the first line of a paragraph to indicate the start.

Insight

Paragraphs do not have to be of uniform size. Like sentences, you can vary their length. A long paragraph, followed by a short one gives a very different tempo to the rhythm of the words and breaks up the pattern on the page, making it more interesting for the eye.

Layout and design

The look of a document is just as important as the words that are written within it. The format is like a shop window or stage, displaying the words to best effect. If the layout is pleasing to the eye, it is easier to read.

The majority of writers use a computer. That means we have a huge array of design tools at our fingertips: different styles, fonts, colours, themes, tables, graphics. The temptation is to throw everything at our words to give them a bit of zip. Unless you are a qualified designer, the best approach is show a bit of restraint.

▶ The aim is to make your words intelligible *and* visually appealing.

- ▶ If it looks good, it helps the reader take in what you are saying.
- ▶ If you have too much visual 'noise' going on, it can be confusing and get in the way of your message.
- ▶ Wall-to-wall text can be off-putting.
- ▶ White space helps give contrast between the background and the text making the words easier to read.

GRAPHICS

Graphics should add to the written words and not just replace them. If you are going to use graphics in your work, make sure they are situated near the text that they refer to. It is frustrating to have to flip over pages (either hard copy or on screen) to match up the text with the graphic.

Even if you have the graphic placed next to or near the relevant text, make sure you refer to it in the words, for example: 'see Illustration 3'. Point your reader in the right direction at all times.

MARGIN AND COLUMN WIDTHS

The default setting for most documents on a computer is 24mm margins at the sides, top and bottom. Wide margins make a document more readable. The shorter the line of text to read, the easier it is for the reader's eye to jump from one end of a line to the start of the next. Conversely, the longer the line, the more effort required to move from one line to another.

When you are setting up your document:

- ▶ make the left margin at least 2.5 cm (1 inch) and the right margin 1.25 to 2.5 cm (½ inch to 1 inch)
- ▶ the top and bottom margins should be 2.5 cm (1 inch).

This frames the text on the page.

FONTS

The shape of letters gives an added, subtle meaning to what we write. Readers respond to the shape and look of the text, just as much as they do to the meaning of the words. When you pick your font, you are sending out a signal. Readers will be drawing their own conclusions from the typeface. Use Comic Sans? Are you trying to say you are fun, wacky and a bit off the wall? Or do you use Times New Roman to be taken seriously?

Fonts come in two main types:

- ▶ serif (little details on the ends of letters and symbols) such as: Palatino, Garamond
- ▶ sans serif (plain) such as: Arial, Helvetica.

Most printed newspapers and many magazines use a serif font, the belief being that the lines on the ends of the letters lead the eye and aid fast reading. Sans serif fonts have become popular in recent times due to the advent of online and onscreen technology. Because the resolution of the letters is not as high onscreen as it is in print, it is easier for the eye to take in sans serif fonts. The same online papers use a sans serif font. Your computer has a huge list of fonts to choose from and it is tempting to go for something a bit different. But before you do, consider your reader first. There are nearly 200 typefaces available on your computer, some more legible than others. Quirky, odd fonts can be extremely difficult to read – even for people with decent eyesight.

Font size

The size of fonts is measured in 'points' (pt). So you will hear reference to 9 pt, 14 pt and so on. Sizes 11 and 12 pt are good for most readers; those sizes don't take up too much space but are not so small as to make the words difficult to read. You can go down to 10 pt if space is at a premium but anything smaller than that can be hard to decipher for main text.

If you are writing for a specific audience that may have difficulty reading small text, you can tailor your print size to them. In the UK, there are 2 million people with sight problems. The RNIB (Royal National Institute of Blind People) suggests 9–12 pt as the absolute minimum for partially sighted readers; 14 pt is better while printed documents (like large print books) use 16 pt. If you are unsure of your audience's specific requirements, it is best to be flexible.

Titles, headings and subheadings

Use them to help direct your reader's attention. They act as signposts, giving the reader a glimpse of the content and follow the thread of your message. They should explain the 'who, what, where, how and why'. They are particularly important in academic essays and formal reports.

Newspaper headline writers are masters of their art; they have to compress the most important parts of a story into a few words in order to engage the reader. The skill is so highly regarded that in the US, headline contests, sponsored by the American Copy Editors Society (www.copydesk.org), take place each year (previous winners have included: 'Borders turns last page', 'Health? There's an app for that' and 'Biographer unlocks The Doors'). Not every writer has to come up with an attention-grabbing front page one-liner but writing any effective title requires some thought.

A title is usually the last thing to be written, after the main body of the text. To write a good title:

▶ read and review the content
▶ identify the tone (serious, light-hearted, etc.)
▶ what is the significance or angle of the piece?
▶ where will the title/headline appear (in a report, front page of a newsletter)?
▶ subject – verb – object is often the easiest and best format for a title/headline
▶ keep the structure straightforward; don't make it too complex
▶ be concise and specific.

Insight

If you are finding it difficult to come up with a title, read through the first paragraph again. You can often lift something useful from here. Don't repeat the phrase verbatim; tweak it slightly.

There are three basic styles of writing titles:

▶ **sentence title** – The title of this book (popular for subheadings)
▶ **title case** – The Title of This Book (main headings)
▶ **upper case** – THE TITLE OF THIS BOOK (hard to read and equivalent to shouting).

Whichever style you use, keep it consistent throughout your writing.

▶ For subheadings, capitalize the first word and then use lower case for everything else.
▶ Capitalize the first and last word in a title, as well as all important words in that title. You can use lower case for less important words (a, an, the, but, among, between).

- Use capitals for words of four or more letters (whether prepositions, conjunctions, etc.).
- Capitalize verbs and pronouns, even if they are short (is, be, he, she, etc.).
- Capitalize both parts of a hyphenated compound (such as 'Cease-Fire').

SUBHEADINGS

Subheadings are also useful in that they break up text into readable chunks and make the look of the page more interesting and appealing. Give them space to do their job; most headings stand out more if surrounded by white space (i.e. put a line break above and below).

Careful planning of your subheadings will show the reader at a glance the thrust of your argument or flow of thought. Make sure the subheadings are quite clear about what is in the following section so the reader knows what to expect.

Try to keep a consistency about the subheadings. If you start with a sentence fragment for a subheading, make sure all subheadings are sentence fragments. It also makes the words easier to scan if you start subheadings with the same part of speech (such as a verb or noun).

Most documents will have a main title, headings, then subheadings. There is a distinct order of visual importance. You should keep to the order to help guide your reader. So, headings may be in bold, 14 pt, while subheadings could be in italic and 12 pt.

- Anything more than three levels of headings can get confusing.
- If you find you are getting too many types of headings, revise your work.
- Keep the signposting clear and do not chop and change throughout the document.

Insight

Try making subheadings questions ('What did we find?', 'What do we do now?'). This can give a more conversational feel to the piece and helps you to write clear answers in a direct way in each section.

PUNCTUATION OF TITLES AND HEADINGS

Full stops are rarely used in headings. A question mark is fine as long as a question is being asked. An exclamation mark is best avoided; use strong words instead to give expression and emphasize meaning.

If you are naming the title of a magazine, a book, CDs/DVDs, plays, a newspaper, a film, you need to indicate which of the words are the title. You can:

▶ put the title in quote marks – 'The New York Times'
▶ or use italics – *The Washington Post* – the preferred style in this book.

The second option is more popular now. People used to <u>underline</u> titles but that was in the days of typewriters and has pretty much fallen out of fashion (it can also be confused with active links on a computer screen). Although, underlining titles can still be useful when writing by hand, e.g. in an exam situation.

If you are writing about a poem, a short story, an essay, a chapter in a book or report, a magazine article or an individual episode of a television series, use quotation marks, for example: 'Punctuation' in *The Writer's Guide to Good Style*.

Captions

Captions are the text that appears below an illustration or photograph. Some academic and scientific journals have long captions, often several sentences long, that stand alone in meaning from the main text. Others, such as newspapers and magazines, can be quite brief and the reader will find more explanation in the main body of text.

Whether long or short, a caption should draw the reader's attention to the image, making clear its relevance to the text.

The Economist's Style Guide states that captions:

> *...set the tone; they are more read than anything else, especially in a newspaper. Use them, therefore, to draw readers in, not repel them. That means wit (where appropriate), not bad puns; sharpness (ditto), not familiarity (call people by their last names, not their first names); originality, not clichés.*

Quotations and speech

Direct speech can add life to your prose. It is obviously used more for fiction than non-fiction. But if you are writing dialogue, or quoting multiple sources one after the other, it is important that the reader knows who is speaking. A speech or quotation generally goes before the name of the person who is speaking ('We should be able to see now,' said Helen).

If you are quoting another source, you should put quotation marks round the direct words. Anything inside the quotation marks is then assumed to be the actual words written (or spoken). There is more information on punctuation and quotation marks in Chapter 2.

Visuals

What a lot of these visual elements do is create a hierarchy of information. You can divide the major points from the less important ones and streamline information into one or two visual points so that it helps guide the reader through your argument.

Let's take a look at the various tools you can use to format your copy:

BOLD, ITALICS, UNDERLINING

These graphic devices all help draw the reader's attention to key words. Use separately and sparingly; overuse dulls the effect.

- ▶ **Boldface** – helps readers to focus on important words (such as key terms, a heading or a one word/phrase in a sentence). Useful in documents that the reader only scans quickly, such as flyers, adverts and CVs.
- ▶ *Italics* – use for titles (newspapers, films, albums), foreign words and phrases that have not passed into common usage, and to make the odd word stand out. Don't write whole paragraphs or pages in italics. It is hard for readers to make out.
- ▶ Underlining – not as popular as it used to be because an underlined word looks like an active link on a website.

WHITE SPACE

What you leave out is just as important as what you put in. White space gives the reader's eye a rest from all the text, illustrations and graphics. Look at the margins of this book; imagine what the page would be like if they weren't there. The pages would be crowded with words, wall-to-wall text. It would be off-putting and far too much to take in.

LEADING (PRONOUNCED 'LEDDING')

This is the space between lines of type. Measured in the same units as font size, it should be one and a half to two times the space between words on a line. So, for body text of 10 pt, you would have a leading of 12 pt (which is the default setting on computers). For your main text, the leading should be greater than the space between words; otherwise it can be hard for the reader to follow the text.

LINE LENGTH

This can affect the speed at which people read and the ease with which they navigate through the text. Very long or short lines slow readers down; they have to concentrate on what they are reading. That is not necessarily a bad thing if there is a message that you want to make sure your reader reads. Measure your line length by the number of characters there are in a line (including any spaces). Generally, a line of text should have between 60–72 characters (about ten words).

ALIGNMENT

Unjustified text (aligned to the left margin) gives the ragged, uneven finish to lines of text on the right hand side of the page.

This paragraph is **justified**. Justified stretches the text out so each line is the same length. It may look neater but the spacing between words varies which can make it hard for some people to read (especially those with visual impairments). If you align your text to the left margin, it is easy for readers to find the start and finish of each line.

LISTS

Lists are extremely reader-friendly. They divide information into easily read and understood clauses. They break up the text on the page so that there is more white space.

You can find lists in all kinds of writing: from Teach Yourself books to finance reports. And they flag up to the reader that here is some useful information. Lists also encourage the writer to keep things brief, rather than use long sentences.

You can write lists within sentences: 'We drove through several major cities: London, Bristol, Cardiff and Birmingham.' In which case, keep them fairly short; no more than three or four items to a list. Or you can lay them out using the styles below.

- ▶ **Bullet points** – simple and straightforward to read. Use when the order of the items in the list doesn't matter (if in doubt, put the list in alphabetical order). You can use the traditional solid round circle or choose a different form from the bullet library on your computer.
- ▶ **Lettered lists** – a, b, c, etc. Use these when you either want your reader to make a choice from the list or you need to refer back to one of the items later. Lower case letters are more acceptable than upper case.
- ▶ **Numbered lists** – use when the sequence is important (as in a recipe, describing a process or sequence of events). If you have more than 15 items in your list, put them into a table for greater readability.

Try to avoid having list within lists. You have to change bullet point style (or numbering/lettering) and the layout can get really confusing. A good list should:

- ▶ have an introduction; let the reader know why the list is important
- ▶ start each new item with a different action verb (don't repeat the verb throughout)
- ▶ list each item separately
- ▶ keep to a logical order
- ▶ not mix styles (i.e. use either complete sentences or sentence fragments/single words)
- ▶ use the active voice rather than the passive if possible (see Chapter 4 for more information on use of the active/passive)
- ▶ be fairly short; not a huge long list that goes on and on.

Punctuating lists

If you start your list with an introductory sentence, put a colon at the end of that sentence to introduce the list, like this:

- ▶ If each point in a list is a complete statement, start with a capital letter and end with a full stop.
- ▶ If the list is made up of sentence fragments, you do not need to add end punctuation (such as commas, full stops, etc.) and you can start each new point with lower case letters.

- ▶ If the list is a continuous statement, you can put commas (or semicolons if each item is a bit more involved) after each point if you want to; leaving them out makes the list less fussy.
- ▶ Be consistent.

For lists that are continuous statements, some writers like to put 'and' (or 'or' depending on the meaning) after the semicolon; others prefer to leave it out. You don't have to do it; it's a matter of style and preference. If anything, the trend is not to do it because it adds unnecessary clutter to the page. For example:

- ▶ When you go abroad, you should always take:
    - ▷ your passport;
    - ▷ foreign currency or traveller's cheques; *and*
    - ▷ your insurance details.

What you must do is make sure your list follows a logical and grammatical order. For example:

- ▶ When he went to college, Callum wanted:
    - ▷ to get on the football team
    - ▷ join the drama club
    - ▷ to be top of his class.

In this example, the second bullet point does *not* follow on grammatically from the introductory sentence. If you ignored the other two bullet points and added it to the end of the sentence it would read: 'When he went to college, Callum wanted join the drama club.' It needs an infinitive, like the other two points ('*to* join the drama club'). All the parts of the list need to have the same grammatical identity as each other; this is called parallel construction, i.e. each item in the list is a continuation of the introductory sentence. Make sure your tenses are the same throughout as well; if you start with the present tense, the tenses in your list must be present tense as well.

When proofreading lists, make sure that:

- ▶ they begin and end the same way
- ▶ a top ten list has ten items
- ▶ if alphabetical, everything is in alphabetical order
- ▶ if numbered, everything is in numerical order.

These are useful to show large amounts of data in a straightforward manner, such as display results, show progress and identify opportunities. Most software programs now allow you to display information in charts, tables and graphs at the touch of a button. Here are some tips to make the most of tables and graphs:

▶ Give the chart, table or graph a clear, descriptive title.

▶ If it's not clear, explain what the sections in the graphs/tables/ charts represent.

▶ Make sure the scale is appropriate to the data shown; for example, if the chart shows measurements in centimetres, don't have the range in metres.

▶ If you can just use tabulation (tabs), then don't put the information in a table; keep it simple.

▶ If you have a long list in your chart, consider using alternating shaded lines to break up the information and make it easier to read.

▶ Be prepared to have more than one table or chart, rather than try to cram all the information onto one.

▶ Keep it simple.

Numbers

Charts, tables and graphs are excellent tools for representing numbers in clear, easily understood formats. Many people are worried by numbers, especially if they are not used to using them on a regular basis. So a writer needs to take this into account when working with and presenting numbers. In this book, we refer to 'numerals' (which represent actual figures: 1, 35, 189) and 'written numbers' (numbers written out in full, up to ten: one, three, five, eight, etc.).

▶ When using numbers, keep a consistent style; don't mix numerals (such as 2 and 3) with written numbers (such as 'four' and 'five').

▶ Cardinal numbers: describe quantity (1, 2, 3, etc.) and can answer the question 'how many?'

▶ Ordinal numbers: describe position (first, second, third, etc.) and indicate an order.

- ▶ Use numerals if you are stating a sequence of quantities: 'The figures for the year show an increase of 546,000 units; a 13% uptake on the year before.'
- ▶ If you are writing about units of measurement (distance, volume, weight, time, force, etc.) use numerals.
- ▶ Separate objects are not units of measurement unless you are representing them statistically: 'We have three cats, two dogs and ten chickens.'
- ▶ When describing numbers under 100, you generally use written numbers ('Twenty ships, fifteen submarines and twelve helicopters'), but this is a question of style. Anything over 100 is written as numerals. Note that in newspapers, and publishers such as this one, numbers one to nine are usually written as words, but ten and above are given as numerals.
- ▶ Express large and very large numbers in numerals followed by million, billion and so forth: '5 billion', '10 million'.
- ▶ If space is tight, use numerals for all numbers, particularly in headlines, email subject lines and HTML page titles.
- ▶ Avoid starting sentence with a figure if possible. If you can't avoid it, spell it out: 'Four hundred and fifty men...' – not '450 men...'. It is absolutely fine to start a headline with a figure if space is tight or it makes the title more eye-catching.
- ▶ For unrounded numbers, only figures will do so write 3,978,665 rather than three million, nine hundred and seventy-eight thousand, six hundred and sixty-five. At the lower end, make a rule for yourself – stick to it about where to stop using words and start using numbers/figures.

If you treat numbers consistently, your readers can recognize the relationship between them more easily.

Be aware that there are global differences in the way that people write numbers. In the UK, people use a comma in most whole numbers of four or more digits – 30,000 pounds, $1,500. But many other countries use the International System of Units in which spaces are used in numbers with five or more digits, for example: 30 000 pounds. In the US and the UK, they use a decimal point (.) but in continental Europe, a comma is often the decimal separator, for example: €20,00 = £20.00

DATES

It is more usual to write '3 September 1939' nowadays rather than '3rd September 1939'; the abbreviation ('rd' for 'third', 'st' for 'first' or 'th' for numbers like 'seventh') is gradually being dropped. Putting the day's date before the month keeps it separate from the numbers of the year and so avoids confusion and an untidy mess of numbers (September 3 1939).

▶ If you are referring to two dates you can either put 'to' between or a dash ('from 1989 to 1990' or 'from 1989–1990'); it's a matter of personal preference and style. Just be consistent in your use.

▶ If you are abbreviating a date (3/9/39) be aware that there are differences in how countries read them. In the US, this would be seen as 9 March 1939; while in the UK, it would be read at 3 September 1939.

Colours

Most of the time, we write our copy in black on a white background, which is easy to read. Computers and colour printers allow us to add some colour to our writing.

Colours also play a part in how words are presented; they can help emphasize meaning. Research has shown that:

▶ Cool colours, such as blues and greys, suggest dependability and trust – ideal for a business-like appearance.

▶ Blues are used widely to represent something medical or clinical.

▶ If you want more fun and excitement, use warm colours such as reds, oranges and yellows.

▶ Greens and browns work for an environmental, organic feel.

▶ Browns and yellows are safe and comfortable.

▶ Black, grey, metallic are elegant, lasting, wealthy looking.

How much is too much?

Computers have made us designers as well as writers. We can format our work at the touch of a button. Sometimes, it is almost too easy to make changes, and the choice is overwhelming. Unless you are a trained graphic designer, practise restraint. The aim is to make your words clear and easy to read – not get in the way of your message.

Once you have got the look right, you can think about how to address your reader. Understanding who you are writing for is a crucial element of planning your work. This is what we will be looking at in Chapter 4.

10 THINGS TO TRY

1 Find a passage that you think is unclear. Look at the length of the sentences and paragraphs. What is the average length? Can you make more sense by shortening the sentences and paragraphs?

2 Take a story from the newspaper and rewrite it using sentence fragments. See if you can keep the sense and meaning.

3 Play around with the sentence length in a piece of writing; make it as long as possible and then break it up into shorter segments. See how it changes the tone and rhythm.

4 Take a piece of writing (fiction or non-fiction) and identify the main arguments or changes in the story and give it subheadings. Can you follow the flow and get an understanding of the content? If not, where should the subheadings be changed?

5 Take something you have written (it could be formal or informal). Play around with different fonts; study the effect a sans serif font has as opposed to a serif font. Which one suits the subject matter of the writing?

6 Read your work out loud; it is a good way to check whether your sentences are too long or not. If you run out of breath, you should look at splitting the sentence.

7 Start to build a library of titles. Look at titles and headings in what you are reading. Could you improve on what is there?

8 Look at a factual piece of writing: can you present some of those facts in a graph or table? What sort of graph is best to show off the figures?

9 Do the same with the information but present it in a list format. Which style is best?

10 Have a go at writing a haiku. The subject could be about anything at all. It should be made up of three lines, with five syllables on the first line, seven on the second and five on the last line.

4

Writing for an audience

In this chapter you will learn:
- **the difference between writing formal and informal English**
- **how to plan what to write**
- **to work out who your readers are**
- **how to pitch your words at the right level.**

> **The difficulty is not to write, but to write what you mean, not to affect your reader, but to affect him precisely as you wish.**
>
> Robert Louis Stevenson

This chapter looks at all the elements a writer needs to take into consideration before starting to write. Writing is about communication; you are 'talking' to your reader. It is therefore important to have the reader at the forefront of your mind as you plan and then start to write.

We don't communicate the same way all the time; it depends on who we are talking to or writing for. Between friends, our language is informal, probably full of slang, repetition and loose sentence structure. It doesn't really matter if we make mistakes. Whereas talking or writing to our boss, bank manager or a stranger sees a shift in the language we use. We are much more careful with the words and tone. Think of your writing as one half of a conversation. What tone and style is appropriate to the conversation you are having?

For the purposes of this book, we will roughly divide writing into conversational or informal and formal English. When we refer to informal or formal English, we mean:

▶ **Conversational or informal English** – used in emails, blogs, chat rooms, letters to friends and relatives, even memos to some colleagues. You can use contractions (don't, can't, won't), relaxed punctuation, short sentences, abbreviations and colloquialisms. This is writing how people speak.

▶ **Standard or formal English** – is the most common type of English found in print. It sticks by the rules; you do not generally write as you would speak. Tone is important; formal English is used for business letters and emails, letters to officials; reports; homework; essays; speeches; presentations. It contains subordinate clause sequences and complex phrases.

There is a place for both styles. It would be ridiculous to send out a Christmas round robin letter, written in the style and tone of an annual business report and vice versa. It is all about the appropriateness of the tone. And the greater your ability to change your tone (in the appropriate places) the better for you as a writer because it means you can communicate at all levels.

Insight

Don't mix the two styles (formal, informal) in the same text. It sends out mixed messages which is confusing for the reader. Both formal and informal writing requires thought and care. The more effort you put into it, the easier it is to read and understand.

What are your objectives?

You should have an idea of what you want to say before you write anything. Write down what your objectives are. Do you want to create awareness of something? Do you want to change or influence people's attitudes? Do you want to make a statement? Ask yourself:

▶ What do I want to achieve from this?
▶ Is it a follow-up to something or a written record?
▶ Do I need to inform the reader of something?
▶ Do I want to persuade the reader to do something?
▶ Do I want them to respond and if so, how?
▶ What do I want the reader to do after they have read it?

Who is your audience?

You are dealing with people when you write, not just writing about a solution or a situation. Put yourself in the position of the person receiving the communication. Anticipate their needs, wishes, interests and problems.

Are they busy people with precious time to spare? Then don't send a long email. Should you throw long words at a learned readership? Dumb down to others? Can you anticipate what mood they will be in when they read your document?

What does the reader *need* to know? It is not about telling them everything *you* know. For example, if you are writing for managers or directors, they usually want to know the big picture; sales people and customers want the benefits; while technical people want details. Ask yourself:

▶ Who is my reader?
▶ What do they already know about the subject?
▶ What do they need to know?
▶ How will they respond (receptive, hostile, indifferent, objective)?
▶ How much time do they have?
▶ What information do they need?
▶ What is their level of understanding?

Answer these questions and you start to get an idea of how long your document should be, what information it should include, as well as its tone, style and structure.

Writing to one or many?

A letter to your grandmother is easy; a report to the Board of Directors – again, you know who will be reading your words. If you are writing to a group of people, with a shared interest or knowledge, you can focus on one person (real or imagined) and address your words to them. But if the audience is a diverse one, then it is much more difficult to target the core group.

You could argue, for instance, that just about anyone, anywhere in the world, could read your website. How can you write for such a wide readership? The trick is to concentrate on the core group of that audience. Who is the primary audience? What do the secondary readers need to know? The advantage of this is that you stop thinking of the readers as a vague mass and begin to see them as real people. It gives your writing focus. Write to 'everyone' and you run the risk of producing bland words that speak to no one.

▶ **Primary readers** – those people who have the greatest need to receive the information and act upon it.

▶ **Secondary readers** – may have the same interest in what you are writing but do not need the same kind of detail. They need the information but are not necessarily going to be the ones to act on it.

Insight

Even when you are writing reports, presentations and websites aimed at more than one person, have someone in mind when you start planning and then writing; it can be a real person or an imaginary individual. This helps to give focus to your work and keep your writing on track.

Whatever you write, you need to think like your reader; what would they expect? To do that, you need to know who they are and what they expect. If you are not entirely sure who that core group or main reader is, you need to do some research. Ask yourself:

▶ How old are your readers?
▶ What do they do (student, business people, retired, employed/unemployed)?
▶ What is their education?
▶ Are they male/female?
▶ What is their income?
▶ Where do they live?
▶ What are their political or religious views
▶ What newspaper do they read?

If it is a business document, it may be worth conducting some research: interview people, run surveys. The answers (even if you have made them up because you are imagining the type of reader) will help you. You start to see the reader as a real person and that helps the way you write. Remember:

▶ that common words are easily understood by the majority of readers
▶ to spell out shortened words if writing for a general readership (e.g. 'statistics' rather than 'stats'; 'specification' rather than 'spec')
▶ to avoid slang and idiom.

Vigorous writing is concise. A sentence should contain no unnecessary words, a paragraph no unnecessary sentences, for the same reason that a drawing should have no unnecessary lines and a machine no unnecessary parts. This requires not that the writer make all his sentences short, or that he avoid all detail and treat his subjects only in outline, but that every word tell.

William Strunk & E B White *The Elements of Style*

64

Planning what to write

Thinking about what you are going to write is as important as what you write. It is difficult to think and write at the same time, especially if you are not a professional writer – and even they have to go back and edit what they write.

....

Insight
Before you write anything, write your message in a single, precise sentence. If you can sum it up in one sentence, it helps focus your mind on what you want to achieve.

....

There are several stages to planning and writing.

What do you want to communicate?
Work out what your message is going to be.

Gather information
Have the facts ready before you write. Even a letter complaining about refuse collection can benefit from a bit of forward planning; check your diary for the relevant dates; work out who to send the letter to. It is easier to write with the facts to hand, rather than trying to write and research at the same time.

Thinking
Some would call this procrastination, putting off the moment of writing. But having a think about what you then want to say in your writing is a good idea. Let the ideas percolate and distil in your head before committing them to page or screen.

Make a list
Write down the points you want to make. At this stage, it doesn't matter if they are not in order, the layout is all wrong and the spelling, grammar and punctuation is not spot on, just write them down as they occur to you.

Planning
Now work out the order and outline of what you want to write. Put your points in a logical order (important if you are arguing a point or trying to get someone to see your point of view). Try to keep the list of points as short as possible – enough so that you achieve your aim but not so many that you run the risk of losing your reader in an avalanche of facts.

Writing

This may sound self-explanatory, but when you finally start writing, it may be the first draft of several. Follow the order you have drawn up and just write. You are not aiming for a stream of consciousness, nor are you carefully checking your grammar and punctuation at this point.

Editing

Leave this until after you have written your first draft. Then go back and see if there is anything you want to take out, change or add in. Check the tone and style. Have you got that right?

Write again

For your second draft, make the necessary adjustments.

Polish and proofread

You may need to go to a third draft (or more) but this allows you to polish off any rough edges.

> *Thinking is the activity I like best, and writing is simply thinking through my fingers.*
>
> Isaac Asimov

WHAT TO INCLUDE

The elements of your writing should broadly include:

- ▶ **introduction/statement of purpose** – why you are writing and/ or what you are writing about
- ▶ **background/explanation** – outline of what you are going to write (keep the reader in mind)
- ▶ **summary/conclusion** – summing up the main points you have written
- ▶ **call for response/action** – what you expect from your audience now.

The advantage of all this planning is that you give yourself a clear map of where you want to go, so you and your reader will not get lost along the way. Preparation helps the structure of what you write.

CONTENTS PAGE

You will not need a contents page for every piece of writing. This book has one but a letter or email would not. A short document, with good subheadings, would not need a contents page either. If you have a document that you think your reader will not read all the way through, a contents page can help take them to the parts that they are most interested in.

Addressing the reader

Directly address the reader, either as 'you' or 'we' depending on who you are writing for. It is less formal and cold than 'the workforce', 'the applicant', 'the reader'. It lets them know that there is a person behind the words.

If you are writing for and about a company or organization that you represent, use 'we' or 'I'. Again, it is less formal and gives a more approachable feel. The more formal you are, the more distance you create between you and the reader.

Insight

A complicated idea does not need complicated language, grammar and sentence structure to convey its meaning. Shorter sentences and phrases can sometimes be best when you are trying to explain something complicated.

DEVELOPING TONE AND VOICE

Companies pour millions of pounds and dollars into advertising and marketing their products so that consumers will buy their own brand of goods. For a writer, their 'voice' is their brand. The publishing world knows how important it is to have a distinctive voice in commercial (business) writing and fiction. The reader knows where they are when they pick up a book by Joanna Trollope or Stephen King. They may not even look at the blurb on the back of the book to find out what the story is about; the fact that they know the writer's brand, they know their voice, is enough. Whatever you write, whether it is fiction, letters or company brochures, you should also work on developing your own writing voice.

The brand reflects who you are, either as an individual or as an organization. Are you solid, upstanding and reliable? Or are you fun, funky and a bit wild? Then you need to reflect that in what you write (using the right vocabulary, style and layout).

The tone of voice should also be suitable for your audience and your subject matter/message. The tone of a piece of writing is not quite the same thing as a writer's voice but the two are related; it is the manner in which you use your writer's voice on paper.

▶ Voice = personality
▶ Tone = mood / attitude

VOICE CHART

What qualities can your voice have? To work out what your writing voice is, you should draw up a voice chart. Write down a load of descriptive words that you feel describe your voice. Use words such as:

conservative	matter-of-fact	cheerful	humorous
quirky	serious	caring	sympathetic
trendy	funky	professional	upbeat
apologetic	unapologetic	provocative	formal
informal	friendly	reserved	edgy

Once you have a good mix, narrow it down to about four or five descriptive words that you feel encompass your writer's voice. You don't want so many words that you could be describing anyone or too few that don't give a full enough picture; four or five will be fine to give a full picture of what you are after. You can be trendy and upbeat – but are you chatty with it? Earnest or laid back? Or something in between?

With your voice chart in place, you now have the personality for your writing. If you feel you are drifting away from that personality, refer back to the voice chart.

The voice chart can also help guide you to choose the right words to suit your voice; so, for example:

▶ If you are aiming for a traditional, formal voice, avoid using slang.
▶ If you are edgy and very much on trend, you can go for words that aren't actually in a dictionary yet or even make up your own new words.

POSITIVE AND NEGATIVE

Should you be taking a positive or negative attitude? People instinctively dislike being told negative things. We often feel that there is an implied criticism hidden in the negative statements. Nobody likes being told off or criticized and that can happen if a writer continually strikes a negative tone. If you can, always take a positive slant on things.

Avoid phrases and words like:

failed to   you claim   I'm not available   too expensive

Insight

One way to avoid striking a negative tone is to use 'when' rather than 'if'; for example, 'We will give you a raise *if* you meet these goals' is not as positive as 'We will give you a raise *when* you meet these goals.'

It is not always easy, especially if there is bad news to write about, but you can try to turn a negative into a positive. For example:

Negative	Positive
The strategy is not good.	The strategy has drawbacks.
The factory will close on Friday.	The factory will remain open until Friday.
We can't take payments of £5 or less.	We can take payments of £5 and over.
I'm not available until next week.	You can reach me on Monday.

If you want to emphasize a point, put it at the end of the sentence. In this way, you use a positive statement to minimize the sting of a negative one, for example: 'The design has not made it to the final round but we have passed it on to our colleagues at our sister company who may be interested in taking it further.' Notice the 'but' in the middle of the two phrases which separates the negative from the positive; it signals that something better is to follow the negative.

Obviously you cannot avoid using the negative completely, but try to use it in a strategic way. For example, describing negative experiences of potential customers before giving positive solutions to their dilemma.

We touched on the active and passive use of verbs in the first chapter but we will look at the different uses (and the advantages and disadvantages) there are with one or the other in more detail here.

Just to recap briefly, in a sentence that uses the active voice (and therefore an active verb) the subject – verb – object appear in the following order:

▶ The early bird [subject] catches [verb] the worm [object].

'Catches' is the active verb. A sentence that uses the passive voice (and therefore a passive verb) reverses this order so that the object comes before the verb and is followed by the subject:

▶ The worm [object] is caught [verb] by the early bird [subject].

The worm is the receiver of the action (being caught).

Generally, the active voice is livelier, more direct and less wordy, while the passive can be impersonal and detached:

▶ I love the children [active] = the children are loved by me [passive].

Read any James Bond novel and you will find it full of active verbs which seems entirely suitable for an action adventure about a secret agent. Many style books have criticized the passive form declaring it should be avoided at all costs; George Orwell instructed writers to 'Never use a passive when you can use the active.' It is true that the passive form can keep the writer hidden away. It uses more words than the active and, with the move towards a simpler, clearer, more direct English, it is understandable that the active would be preferred.

However, that does not mean you should avoid the passive voice altogether. There is a place for it; it just depends on what you want to say and how you want to say it. In many cases, a passive sentence does not mention who or what did the action. This is ideal if you do not want to say who was responsible for the action, either because you don't know ('the window was broken') or because it is kinder than the more direct (naming someone or thing) active approach ('you broke the window') or because you don't want to take the blame for something ('mistakes were made' rather than 'we made mistakes').

The passive works well in:

▶ a report (business or academic)
▶ technical and scientific writing
▶ giving instructions or
▶ similar documents where a more detached, impersonal approach is suitable.

Unsurprisingly, the passive voice is also quite popular with politicians and corporations who effectively use the evasive quality of the passive voice to distance and depersonalize an action. For example:

▶ 'It is recommended that cuts are made' rather than 'We have to make cuts'.
▶ 'It has been decided to reduce the workforce' rather than 'I am going to sack staff'.
▶ 'Bombs were dropped' instead of 'We dropped bombs'.

While the passive is therefore acceptable, it is a good idea to have a greater percentage of active verbs than passive. Certain versions of Microsoft Word allow you to check your use of passive verbs so you can see whether you are using them too much. However, as with any computer programmes (like spellcheck), it is not 100 per cent reliable so do your own check as well.

TRANSITION WORDS

Transition words are useful to guide the reader through various ideas. Without transition words, the reader would have to keep backtracking to make sense of the text. As you change from one argument to another, or move on to a new topic, use a transition word or phrase ('however', 'as a result') to alert the reader to the change. Think of them as traffic signals:

▶ Red – stopping and changing direction (however, but, on the other hand, yet)
▶ Yellow – slow down (furthermore, coincidentally)
▶ Green – keep going (in fact, first, second, third, for example)
▶ Arriving at your destination – (finally, in conclusion, therefore).

WRITING QUESTIONS

What happens when you ask someone a question? They start thinking of the answer. It is a good way to engage your readers. Using questions in your writing is beneficial because:

▶ you have to put yourself in your reader's shoes and look at things from their angle
▶ readers appreciate that the writer is thinking about them
▶ questions give a more conversational tone to the writing
▶ they give the sense of a two-way conversation between reader and writer
▶ questions help the structure of the piece and guide the reader.

GIVING INSTRUCTIONS

The technical term for instructions (or commands) in a language is the 'imperative'. From one word ('Stop!') to a full sentence ('Please return the form in the envelope provided'), imperatives are pretty straightforward. Yet many writers seem uncomfortable using the imperative. Perhaps they are worried that they will seem abrupt or rude. So they wrap up their commands in flowery or long-winded sentences. 'Customers are advised that they should use the elevator' is a roundabout way of saying 'Use the elevator'.

Keep to the point and avoid being wordy; if there is a concern that the command may seem a bit harsh, you can always add 'Please'.

GENDER NEUTRALITY

In the past, there was a male bias in language. It was accepted that the masculine pronoun (he, his) could be used generically to mean people in general: 'The swimmer may find he struggles in strong currents' – when talking about swimmers in general, rather than referring to a specific male swimmer.

Doctors and bank managers would nearly always be referred to as 'he', nurses and flight attendants as 'she'. In most cases, nowadays, it is reasonable to assume that around 50 per cent of your readership will be female and that nowadays just as many doctors, lawyers and police officers are female. It is therefore not only politically correct but fair to avoid stressing the male gender.

A language spoken in the Pakistani part of Kashmir has four genders. The trouble with the English language is that there is no gender neutral single pronoun (as there is in other languages) that covers both men and women.

> **Did you know?**
> Some people have felt the need for a new, gender neutral pronoun that covers both male and female. Suggestions have been 'En', 'Co', 'Per' and 'Yt'; they have yet to catch on.

There are various ways of getting round the gender problem. First of all, be specific if you can. If you are talking about men or boys, use 'he, him, his' and 'she, her, hers' when referring to women and girls. Let's take a sentence about a doctor seeing patients. There are various gender neutral ways in which it can be written:

▶ His/her – the doctor has to see his or her patients.
▶ Their – the doctor has to see their patients.
▶ Use a hybrid pronoun 'S/he' – S/he has to see her/his patients.
▶ No pronoun – the doctor has to see patients.
▶ Use 'a' or 'the' instead of the pronoun – the doctor has to see a/the patient/s.
▶ Rewrite the sentence – patients are seen by the doctor.

While all the examples work, the last one is perhaps the best option. 'His/her' makes the sentence a bit clumsy and has 'her' as something of an afterthought. 'Their' is slightly better but, to be grammatically pedantic, is plural but referring to a singular noun. The last suggestion is much more straightforward than the others and just as clear.

Insight
Often it is entirely irrelevant to refer to the gender when you are writing about someone. Why describe someone as a 'female driving instructor' or 'male midwife' unless you are specifically writing about their gender and their job? Angelina Jolie has several children but, if you are talking about her as an actor, why refer to her as 'mother of six'?

The majority of gender-specific nouns in English are related to professions. In most cases, you can substitute the male/female version for a neutral alternative. For example:

Actress	Actor
Ad man	Ad executive
Chairman	Chair
Craftsman	Artisan
Policeman	Police officer
Fireman	Firefighter
Forefather	Ancestor
Foreman	Supervisor
Layman	Non-professional
Maiden name	Birth name/former name
Workman	Worker
To man (vb)	To operate, to staff
Manpower	Employees, workforce, personnel, staff
Mankind	Humanity, human race
Newsman	Reporter, journalist
Housewife	Homemaker
Stewardess	Flight attendant

READABILITY OF DOCUMENT

Good, clear writing does not have to be pitched at a high level. What is more important? People understanding what you are writing or showing off what you know?

In 2004, a University of Bath study looked at web pages about diabetes on fifteen internet health sites. It found that people would need a reading ability of an educated 11- to 17-year-old to understand them. This is too demanding for many people.

One in five Americans read at a fifth-grade level (10–11 years of age). Around 12 million people employed in the UK have the reading skills of an 11-year-old or younger. The average reading age of people in the UK is that of an educated nine year old. Around 16 per cent (over 5 million) adults in England are described as functionally illiterate. That means they can understand short, basic text on familiar topics. Anything unfamiliar or with more complicated language they find difficult to comprehend.

74

Readability is all about the success of reading *and* understanding a piece of text. A readability test bases its rating on the average number of syllables per word and words per sentence. The longer and more complicated the words and sentences, the more difficult it can be to understand what has been written. This is something to bear in mind when writing. Have you judged the readability level correctly for your readers?

This short sentence needs a reading age of less than nine years.

This longer sentence, which contains an adjectival clause and polysyllabic words, has a reading age of more than sixteen years.

www.timetabler.com/reading.html

There are various readability tests. While you can work out the formula yourself, it is much easier to let your computer do the work. There is a programme in Microsoft Office that allows you to check your finished copy for its reading level. It uses the Flesch Reading Ease and Flesch-Kincaid Grade Level tests to quantify the readability level. You can use the programme in either Outlook or Word. In the options for spell check and grammar, tick a box which will 'show readability statistics'.

The Flesch-Kincaid test was developed for the US Army to assess the difficulty of its technical manuals. Pennsylvania was then the first state to require that car insurance policies were written at no higher than ninth grade (14- to 15-year-olds) level of reading difficulty using the Flesch-Kincaid formula and other states, government departments and organizations have followed.

The Flesch-Kincaid test is used extensively in education and rates text so the score is roughly equivalent to grade level; for example, if a document scored 8.2, it would show that the text should be understood by the average 8th grade student (13 to 14 years of age). If you are British and come across a test that scores using the American grade level, just add five to get the actual reading age (i.e. 8th grade + 5 = 13 years old).

The Flesch Reading Ease test, on the other hand, uses a different formula so that you are looking for a high score to indicate ease of comprehension. A score of between 90–100 indicates that the text can be understood by an average 11-year-old; while 60–70 can be understood by 13- to 15-year-olds. Anything under 30 is aimed at university graduates. The *Harvard Law Review,* for example, has a general readability score in the low 30s, while *Reader's Digest* is around 65.

Another readability formula is the SMOG test which estimates the years of education needed to completely understand a piece of writing. To get the score for a piece of writing, count the words of three or more syllables in three ten-sentence samples (from the beginning, middle and end of the piece), estimate the count's square root and add three (for US grade level) or eight (for UK age level). If you prefer, you can go to the NIACE website (National Institute of Adult Continuing Education www.niace.org.uk) and download its SMOG calculator which will calculate the readability level of any text that is pasted into it. Most people will understand a readability level of under ten (= ten years of age and younger).

The Fog Index is another well-known test. It uses the formula:

Reading level (grade) = Average number of words in sentences + percentage of words of three or more syllables) × 0.4

It gives the *number of years* of education that the reader would need to understand the text. *The New York Times* and *Wall St. Journal* have a FOG index of 11-12 (years of education); while *The Bible* has a FOG index of 6. Any text that scores above 12 will be difficult for the average reader to comprehend; a score of around 7-8 will be fine for most people.

The following are reading age scores for various newspapers and books:

To Kill A Mockingbird	11½
A Tale of Two Cities	13
The Sun	14
The Daily Express	16
The Telegraph, The Guardian	17
Financial Times	17½

Organizations usually pitch text for adults at around the 14- to 15-year-old level. If the readership is likely to include a lot of people with poor reading skills, then they drop the level down to 12 to 13 years.

Helping your readers

The Second Edition of the *Oxford English Dictionary* lists over 171,000 words in full use with over 47,000 obsolete words. Over half are nouns, a quarter are adjectives and a seventh are verbs, with the rest being made up of exclamations, conjunctions, prepositions, suffixes and so on. There is quite a lot to choose from.

As readers, we do not like to be misled, confused or unbalanced. Where is the pleasure in struggling through a sentence, finally getting to the end, only to realize that you are no wiser than when you started it? The best way to avoid annoying those readers is to make reading your words as effortless as possible. Then your readers won't have to struggle with what you have written to get some meaning or pleasure from it. To do that, you have to know how to put your thoughts and ideas across clearly and concisely.

In the next chapter, we will look at areas which can muddle and confuse your writing. Chapter 5 is all about what *not* to do.

10 THINGS TO TRY

1 Test the readability of your own writing. Do the same for a piece of work that you admire.

2 Read through any business communications or official letters or memos that you have received. Is the message clear? Have they hit the right note for the reader (you)?

3 Analyse a piece of writing that you admire; is it written in the active or passive voice? Circle the verbs and work out the percentage of active to passive.

4 Read text that quotes a politician; note how many occasions the passive voice is used. Change into the active and see what the difference is.

5 Compare the 'voice' of two different papers reporting on the same story (e.g. a sports story). What is different? Headings, length of words, etc.?

6 Take a piece of your writing that you have written in the past tense. Change the verbs to the present tense. Does it change the tone of the piece?

7 Read your work out loud. Does it 'sound' like your voice? Are you hitting the right tone?

8 Write down the key point of what you are about to communicate in one sentence.

9 Devise a voice chart of your own.

10 Look for negative phrases in your writing and what you read; can you rewrite the words in a positive way?

5

What to avoid

In this chapter you will learn:
- *how to avoid jargon and gobbledygook*
- *how to avoid clichés and tautology*
- *how to avoid wordiness and padding.*

> *Your writing is both good and original; but the part that is good is not original, and the part that is original is not good.*
>
> Samuel Johnson

Sometimes it seems as if writers are trying to be as incomprehensible as possible. Do they fear that if they write in a clear, straightforward and concise style they will be judged harshly by their peers? Does filling their text with long words make them look more intelligent or less? Pretentiousness and obscurity win over clarity and conciseness – and that is not a good thing.

Local councils, corporations, providers of public services, estate agents and lawyers to name a few seem to produce some of the worst examples, full of clichés, jargon and incomprehensible passages. We no longer 'use' things, we 'utilize' them; projects are 'commenced', rather than 'begun'; previews are 'sneaked', agreements are 'hammered out' and bans are always 'slapped' on us. And 'thinking outside the box' seems the norm. If the main aim of writing something is to communicate ideas and inform the readers, there are a lot of times when writers miss that aim.

So far, the book has dealt with what a writer *should* do, the rules and conventions to observe when writing. This chapter is about what *not* to do; the things to avoid or be wary of that, if allowed to creep into the text, can confuse or annoy your readers.

Dangling modifiers

- They post goods to customers wrapped in protective layers.
- Having come down in the lift, the dining room lay in front of us.
- We walked round the cathedral, followed by the art gallery.
- Children who eat sweets often get tooth decay.

There is something not quite right with those sentences. Are the customers wrapped up or their goods? Has the dining room come down in the lift? Was the art gallery following us round the cathedral? And do children who eat sweets *a lot of the time* get tooth decay or do they *often* get tooth decay if they eat sweets?

For most of those examples, it is obvious what the writer was intending. The context helps make the meaning clear. The sentences are just not very elegant rather than completely wrong. It is the last example, the sweet-eating children, where there is ambiguity.

These examples are showing a problem known as 'dangling, missing, unattached or hanging modifiers. A modifier can be a word, phrase or entire clause. They give added meaning (by describing or qualifying) to another element in a sentence. If you place your modifier carelessly, it modifies the wrong word. Then the sentence can be confusing (or amusing) because it is not clear which part of the sentence they are meant to be attached to.

- The boy looking at the book in the corner.

This is ambiguous because it is not entirely clear whether the boy or the book is in the corner.

- The girl in a summer dress walking down the path.

Is it the girl or the dress doing the walking? Obviously the writer meant that the girl was wearing a dress and walking down the path but the way the sentence is laid out gives an odd twist to the meaning. The modifier (or participle) seems to be hanging or dangling in the wrong place.

- Waiting for the bus, the playful kittens fascinated Mrs Jones.

Mrs Jones is the one waiting for the bus and watching the kittens but that is not obvious. As it is written, it could be the kittens waiting for the bus, rather than Mrs Jones.

To rectify the problem, you should either restore the link, putting it as near as possible to the noun or pronoun it modifies, or rewrite the sentence. For example, the above examples now read:

▶ They post the goods, wrapped in protective layers, to customers.
▶ Having got out of the lift, we saw that the dining room lay in front of us.
▶ We walked round the cathedral and then went to the art gallery.
▶ The boy in the corner looking at the book.
▶ The girl, wearing a summer dress, walking down the path.
▶ Waiting for the bus, Mrs Jones was fascinated by the playful kittens.
▶ Children who eat a lot of sweets can get tooth decay.

ONLY, EVEN, AT LEAST

These are adverbs that are used to modify nouns, verbs and other parts of speech. If you are going to use qualifying words like 'only, even' or 'at least' make sure where you position them in the sentence. They are flexible words that can almost be placed anywhere but, in doing so, they subtly alter the meaning. For example, the following sentences all have a slightly different meaning depending on where 'only' is found:

I only went to town to see my sister.	I just wanted to see my sister.
I went only to town to see my sister.	I just went to town and nowhere else.
I went to town only to see my sister.	I went to town to see my sister and nobody else.
I went to town to see my only sister.	I've only got one sister.

Read through what you have written, phrase by phrase, sentence by sentence to make sure your prose makes sense. If you can, leave as much time as possible after you have written before going back and rereading it. Sometimes, distancing yourself from your work allows you to look at it with fresh eyes again. It is easier to pick up mistakes (like dangling modifiers and hanging participles) after some time has passed.

Jargon

Jargon is the specialized or technical language of a trade, profession, or similar group. It is perfectly acceptable if you are writing for people who use it all the time and would therefore definitely understand it. In the right place, jargon is a specialist language and acts as an accurate and effective shorthand.

But all too often, jargon can be pretentious and make writing unnecessarily obscure. Far too many people use jargon to show off; either because they want to look like they belong to a specialist group or because they want to look like they know more than they actually do. And because jargon is so widespread, readers are very good at skimming through it, without taking in its meaning; jargon is easily ignored.

The Plain English Campaign quotes the following example:

> *High quality learning environments are a necessary precondition for facilitation and enhancement of the on-going learning process.*

What the writer is actually trying to say is 'Children need good schools if they are to learn properly.'

Other examples of jargon are:

pre-owned vehicle	used car
negative patient care outcome	death
meaningful statistical downturn	recession
high ranking digital envoy	fax
geographically relocate	transfer/move
a refocusing of the company skill-set	firing people
terminate with extreme prejudice	kill

This is the advantage of keeping your audience in mind. Will they understand your language or not. If you are fairly confident that the majority will understand your technical language (jargon) but acknowledge that there may be a minority that will struggle, you can either:

▶ use the technical term but put a brief explanation in with it (which can take up more space and interrupt the flow)
▶ use a different word or phrase that everybody can understand.

There can be very serious pitfalls to using jargon. During the 7/7 enquiry into the terrorist bombings in London, Lady Justice Hallett, chairing the enquiry, noted that the fire service called a mobile control-room a 'conference demountable unit'. Unsurprisingly, none of the other emergency services knew what this was, causing serious confusion on the day of the tragedy. If you don't speak the lingo, you don't know what is going on. If you write in jargon, your reader won't know what is going on. Don't alienate your audience. Take care to be clear and concise.

Gobbledygook

Gobbledygook is a close relative of jargon; it is another name for words and phrases that fail to communicate clearly. Bureaucratese or double-speak also fall into this category. Successful communication is all about using words in such a way that they mean more or less the same to the reader as well as the writer. That cannot be said of gobbledygook. Gobbledygook is where teachers become 'educators' and 'classroom managers'; camping is 'wilderness recreation' and 'festive embellishments' are actually Christmas lights.

Michael Shanks, a former chairman to the National Consumer Council of Great Britain, said of gobbledygook that it:

> *...may indicate a failure to think clearly, a contempt for one's clients, or more probably a mixture of both. A system that can't or won't communicate is not a safe basis for a democracy.*

www.plainlanguage.gov

You will have come across double-speak and gobbledygook on many occasions. Here are a couple of examples:

> *Where the combined value of the above payments before actual assimilation remains greater than the combined value of the payments after assimilation, the former level of pay will be protected. These protection arrangements apply to the combined value of payments before and after assimilation, not to individual pay components, excepting the provision relating to retention of existing on-call arrangements.*

"Agenda for Change", Central Manchester and Manchester Children's University Hospitals NHS Trust, 2005

It is a tricky problem to find the particular calibration in timing that would be appropriate to stem the acceleration in risk premiums created by falling incomes without prematurely aborting the decline in the inflation-generated risk premiums.

Attributed to Alan Greenspan

To avoid gobbledygook:

- ▶ Have you explained things clearly?
- ▶ Will your readers understand everything?
- ▶ Do you understand what you have written?

If nothing else, writing plain English is surely easier for both you, as the writer, and your reader.

Insight

The Crystal Mark is an internationally recognized seal of approval for documents written in clear English. The mark appears on over 19,000 different documents in the UK, USA, Denmark, Australia and South Africa. Organizations can apply for the mark from the Plain English Campaign (www.plainenglish.co.uk/crystal-mark.html) for each document they produce.

Slang

Slang used to be classified as the special language of a 'low or vulgar person' but it is now seen as a highly colloquial language. It uses new words or words used in a special way, e.g. currently, slang terms for 'good' are 'wicked', 'awesome' and 'sick'.

Slang and jargon are loosely related because slang is used by a particular group. It can add colour and informality to language but whether it is correct to use it or not depends on the occasion and the audience.

The problem can be that, as with jargon, if you are not in that group, you probably won't understand the meaning (for example, for most people of a certain age 'sick' means 'being ill' and not 'good'). Slang and colloquialisms do not sit easily in formal writing. They can work in humorous or satirical writing and can be appropriate on certain occasions. But slang dates very quickly; what can seem cool and quirky one minute can be very tired and old-fashioned in another.

Idiom

Idiom reflects the state of the language. It refers to what is accepted by convention, rather than by strict grammatical rules. It is not quite the same as overloading a text with slang. In English, we can write about 'odds and ends', 'kicking the bucket' or 'it's raining cats and dogs'. These are colloquial expressions understood by native speakers.

▶ Idiom is not easy to grasp if it is not your first language. You can use idiom in intimate, informal communications; it is not ideal for formal writing.

▶ We use contractions when we speak (it's, can't, won't, doesn't). You can use them in writing where they give an informal, chatty style. Again, they are not usually used in very formal writing.

(i)   Never use a metaphor, simile or other figure of speech which you are used to seeing in print.

(ii) Never use a long word where a short one will do.

(iii) If it's possible to cut a word out, always cut it out.

(iv) Never use the passive where you can use the active.

(v)   Never use a foreign phrase, a scientific word or a jargon word if you can think of an everyday English equivalent.

(vi) Break any of these rules sooner than say anything outright barbarous.

George Orwell, 'Politics and the English Language' 1946

Tautology

A tautology is using different words that mean the same thing; essentially repeating words unnecessarily to convey an idea or meaning. A 'free gift' is a tautology because a gift, by definition, is something given without having to pay for it. Another is 'She gave birth to a *baby* boy'; as opposed to a grown-up boy? Or when someone says of themselves, 'I, myself, personally…' Other examples are:

added bonus	a bonus is an added extra anyway
short summary	a summary is a shortened version of text
foreign imports	import means to bring into the country, therefore they must be from another country

general consensus	any consensus has to be general
a convicted criminal	all criminals have been convicted
planning ahead	planning can only be done in advance of something
disappear from sight	if something disappears, you cannot see it
new innovation	innovation is something new
lonely isolation	isolation means being solitary

The problem lies with the use of the adjectives. Tautologies add nothing to your writing and can even give the impression that you do not know what some of the words mean. If it is possible to cut a word, then do it. For example:

Tautology	Better
absolutely perfect	perfect
big in size	big
combined together	combined
true facts	facts
if and when	if
red in colour	red
final outcome	outcome
personal opinion	opinion
completely full	full
current status	status

Other phrases to avoid:

Past history	PIN number	work tirelessly	actual facts
gather together	stupid fool	absolute certainty	terrible disaster
final conclusion	safe haven	grab hold	new creation
continue to	unexpected	ate hungrily	work colleague
remain	surprise	shout loudly	end result
utmost urgency	added bonus	true fact	stop completely

THE REASON BEING...IS THAT...

The phrase is used when you want to explain something. However, for many writers the tendency is to add 'is' but this is incorrect. The verb 'to be' already exists in the word 'being'. If you use 'is' the sentence would then read 'the reason is is that...'

▶ The reason is that I prefer red wine – correct
▶ The reason being is that I prefer red wine – incorrect

When you read back over what you have written, check through for any redundant words that can be taken out. If you can say the same thing in ten words, rather than twenty, then do so. Often, the message is much clearer for being shorter and to the point.

Clichés

Everybody uses clichés; it is hard to avoid them; especially some words that always seem to go together ('far-reaching consequences', 'audible click', 'severely beaten', 'woefully inadequate', etc.). Some clichés are also tautologies, using additional adjectives where none are needed (as in the above examples).

A cliché, rather like jargon, can be a succinct way of expressing quite a complicated idea. If that is the case, then use a cliché but do so sparingly. They are difficult to understand if English is not your first language. Most of the time, clichés tend to be a sign of lazy and unimaginative thinking, especially if your prose is full of them.

In 2004, the Plain English Campaign conducted a survey to find the most annoying clichés. The top three were:

1 At the end of the day
2 At this moment in time
3 Like (as a form of punctuation)

The survey also gave honourable mention to:

24/7	address the issue	ballpark figure
bottom line	blue sky thinking	it's not rocket science
literally	move the goalposts	pushing the envelope
with all due respect	thinking outside the box	

And some that just won't go away:

quantum leap	leave no stone unturned	sight for sore eyes
nip in the bud	way forward	selling like hot cakes
in a nutshell	hang by a thread	light at the end of the
green as grass	by the skin of your teeth	tunnel
acid test	grind to a halt	if you've got it flaunt it
		point in time

You know it is a cliché if:

▶ you start to write it and know how it ends
▶ it repeats a sound (tried and tested) or rhymes (meet and greet).

If you find yourself with a clichéd phrase in your writing:

▶ Delete the clichéd phrase or words altogether.
▶ Use simple, clear, direct words instead of a cliché.
▶ Give a tired old cliché a different twist so that it becomes new and more original.

Insight

Remember that all clichés once started out as fresh and new. Be wary of using and abusing new catchphrases because they can quickly turn into hackneyed old phrases – clichés by any other name.

Double meanings

If used intentionally, double meanings can be amusing and clever. But often, a double meaning is a mistake on the writer's part. The following are just a few examples where newspaper headline writers forgot that some words have more than one meaning, nouns can be mistaken for verbs and vice versa:

▶ 'Squad Helps Dog Bite Victim'
▶ 'Red Tape Holds Up New Bridge'
▶ 'MacArthur Flies Back To Front'
▶ 'British Left Waffles on Falklands'
▶ 'Eighth Army Push Bottles Up Germans'

Titles and headlines seem especially prone to double meanings. That is because there are no additional clues to let us know whether a word is a verb or a noun. The space limitations of texting and tweeting have the same problem. Always review what you have written, looking at it from as many different angles as possible, before sending out.

Double meanings can also occur when writing for a different English-speaking audience. American English and British English, for instance, will use the same words but that have different meanings.

	US meaning	UK meaning
Banger:	a gang member	old car
Cowboy:	a cowhand	unscrupulous tradesman
Flyover:	ceremonial aircraft flight	elevated section of road
Jock:	slang for an athlete	slang for a Scotsman
Jumper:	pinafore dress	knitted upper body garment
Homely:	unattractive	comfortable

Nominalizations

Technically, a nominalization is an abstract noun. An abstract noun is not a physical object, like a ball or a table, but is the name of a technique, an emotion or a process. Nominalizations are formed from verbs and adjectives; even the word, 'nominalization' comes from the verb 'to nominalize'. For example:

Verb	Nominalization
fail	failure
introduce	introduction
arrange	arrangement

Adjective	Nominalization
creative	creativity
reasonable	reasonableness
precise	precision

All that seems fairly harmless and nominalizations are useful if you are not sure who or what is doing the action or when the subject is unimportant. But the problem is that they get used *instead* of the verbs or adjectives that they come from. If you use lots of nouns, instead of verbs:

▶ sentences become longer and more wordy
▶ the writing can become dull and sound as if nothing much is happening
▶ the verbs you do use are weak ones ('was', 'were').

For example (the nominalizations are in italics):

We had a *discussion* about the job situation.	We discussed the job situation.
There was a *failure* by the Government to solve the problem.	The Government failed to solve the problem.
The company needs to consider a *reduction* of costs.	The company needs to consider reducing costs.
There will be a *stoppage* of the water supply.	The water supply will be stopped.

'Scare quotes'

These are the written equivalent of the two crooked fingers, held up either side of the head, when talking. You do not need to use them; they can become irritating very quickly. Take them away and see if you lose anything from not having them there – probably not.

Intensifiers

An intensifier is meant to intensify or underline the actions of other modifying adverbs (modifying adverb = describes the way an action is done). For example: 'the cat ran *very* fast'. 'Very' is the intensifier.

However, there is a tendency in speech and writing to use far too many intensifiers ('We were *so* excited; it was *very very* thrilling and we *really* loved it') and overuse can weaken your writing. 'It was very, very, very cold' – you can get away with this when talking but not when writing. Many style guides do not approve of them; Strunk & White, in *The Elements of Style,* are not happy with words like 'so', 'really', 'very', 'pretty' and suggest that writers should leave them out altogether.

But these words are very much part of the rhythms and pattern of our speech and writing. It can look odd when they are completely removed because they are part of the English idiom. In certain styles of writing, such as reports and academic essays, they certainly should be kept to the minimum, but in other areas, it feels more natural to leave them in.

The advice here is not to avoid them totally but use them in the right context. If you are aiming for a very natural style of writing, that mirrors everyday speech, then there is a place for them.

ONES TO WATCH

▶ 'It was so, like, amazing, to walk, like, where the film stars did and see, like, where they acted' – 'like' is annoying enough as a verbal tic but quite unforgivable when written down.

▶ There is no need to qualify or intensify words that are already absolute, such as 'unique'.

▶ Be careful when using 'literally' to describe something. 'Literally' means 'in the literal sense' but many writers use it to exaggerate and intensify statements, as in: 'I literally laughed my head off' meaning 'I laughed a lot'. Obviously, the writer's head did not fall off while doing so. In this sense, 'literally' actually means 'figuratively'. It is perhaps best to avoid using 'literally' unless you really mean it.

Mixing British and American English – two nations divided by a common language

There are several distinct differences between the two languages. In *The King's English* (1906), the Fowler brothers wrote that 'The English and American language and literature are both good things but they are better apart than mixed.' Make sure you write with one 'accent' or the other.

Take 'for ever/forever' as an example of the differences between a word. In British English, 'for ever' was always written as two words while it is written as one word in America. We say *was* written because 'forever' is becoming more common on both sides of the Atlantic and that is true of many English versions.

It is getting increasingly difficult to keep the two languages apart, thanks to the influence of television, film and the internet. And there may come a time when the divisions blur and the two become one. But for now, there are still differences and, as the Fowlers suggest, it is best to keep them apart.

▶ You go to the shops in England and pay the bill; you go to the store and pay the check in America.

▶ Men have moustaches in England but mustaches in America.

▶ The British fill forms in; Americans fill forms out.

SPELLING NOUNS AND VERBS

In British English, though not in American, words like 'licence' are spelt one way if they are nouns; if they are being used as a verb, the 'c' becomes an 's': 'license'. If you are British and get confused between the two, remember that 'n' for noun comes before 'v' for verb, just as 'c' comes before 's' in the alphabet. So the noun is spelt with a 'c' and the verb with an 's'. If you are American, you are lucky; you do not have to worry about this distinction.

Other words with the same pattern:

Noun	Verb
advice	advise
defence	defense
device	devise
practice	practise
prophecy	prophesy

SPELLING DIFFERENCES

▶ -ise/-ize – in British English, many verbs now end with -ise; American English uses -ize. -ise was a fashion adopted by the British to distance themselves from US spelling, although -ize has been used in British spelling since the fifteenth century. Certain companies or publications will use one form or the other as their house style. Whichever you use, be consistent throughout your text.

Note: Some verbs, whether in British or American English, always end in -ise (for example: exercise, rise, comprise, merchandise, enterprise, improvise, despise, arise, chastise, advertise, revise, supervise).

▶ Words ending in -our (UK) are usually spelled -or (US), e.g. favour/favor; humour/humor
▶ Words ending in -re (UK) end in -er (US), e.g. theatre/theater; centre/center
▶ -oe/-ae (UK) becomes -e (US), e.g. amoeba/ameba; anaesthetics/anesthetics
▶ Final L – UK spelling has two; US spelling has a single -l, e.g. jeweller/jeweler; travelled/traveled
▶ Endings – UK English tends to end words in the past tense with a -t (learnt, burnt, dreamt); while US English uses -ed (learned, burned, dreamed), though the latter is becoming more prevalent in the UK.

The advice is to stick to one type of spelling, rather than mixing the two. You can set your computer to use UK English spellings or for US English, which should help keep the two styles apart.

DATES

There are differences and they can be confusing. Does 10/11/12 mean 10 November 2012 or 11 October 2012? If you are writing for your home audience (British or American) be consistent and make sure that the dates are clear and not ambiguous. Remember:

▶ British English writes the date: dd/mm/yy.
▶ American English writes the date: mm/dd/yy.

If your audience is potentially international, write the date out in full, e.g. 5 November 1961 rather than 5/11/61 or 11/5/61.

Single/plural nouns

The old rule used to insist that a single verb should always be used with a collective noun but that often led to grammatically correct but rather awkward sounding sentences, e.g. 'None of them is worried'. So the collective noun + single verb rule has been relaxed.

There can be problems when people are not sure whether some collective nouns should be regarded as singular or plural. Should it be 'the majority is winning' or 'the majority are winning'? It can depend on the context of the word itself. If the sense of the sentence is dealing with two individuals, then make it plural; if they are regarded as a unit, make it singular. For example:

▶ 'The couple was greeted at the hotel.' – single verb because the couple is being treated as a single entity.
▶ 'The family were inoculated last week.' – plural verb because the members of the family were given their jabs individually, rather than as a single entity.

Politics, although it has an 's' at the end, is regarded as a single noun (therefore uses the singular form of the verb); the same goes for mathematics, economics, analysis. While scissors, slacks, trousers and headquarters always use the plural.

Time and money are single entities in grammar so need the single form of the verb ('Twenty minutes is ample time; $5,000 is a lot of money'). If you are referring to money in its physical form ('there are twenty £1 coins in the till'), then use the plural verb.

It can also depend which side of the Atlantic you are on; American English tends to regard collective nouns as singular, British English as plural.

▶ American English: The Board was unable to come to a decision.
▶ British English: The Board were unable to come to a decision.

There is a growing tendency (on both sides of the Atlantic) to treat band or team names that sound plural (*The Rolling Stones*) as plural and those that sound singular (*Radiohead*) as singular.

There is no hard and fast rule on this so you can use your own judgement. What gives the right impression? Whichever one you choose (singular or plural) stick to it; do not change from single to plural mid-sentence.

Acronyms

Acronyms are words formed from the initial letters of a group of words. Most acronyms are in upper case letters (NASA, OPEC, ATM) while others have sometimes dropped to lower case (Aids). Some have become so common that they are now words in their own right, such as 'radar' (which originally stood for '**ra**dio **d**etection **a**nd **r**anging') and Nato (North Atlantic Treaty Organization). American English tends to capitalize the whole of the acronym while British English just has the first letter as a capital.

Practically every one of us has sat in a meeting where the speaker has used baffling acronyms. If one brave person asks for the meaning, it is soon becomes clear that a few other people were in the dark as well. Bear that in mind when you are writing that not everyone will know what the acronyms mean.

If there is any possibility of confusion, spell them out. We are not saying you should drop acronyms altogether, use the acronym but then write the meaning out in full in parentheses afterwards. You can then continue to use the acronym knowing that your reader will understand, for example: 'SKU' (shelf-keeping unit).

Abbreviations

Acronyms are a form of abbreviation. If an abbreviation does not form a word (BBC, ITV, IBM, P&O, etc.), then it is not an acronym – just an abbreviation. Many acronyms are perfectly acceptable and familiar abbreviations but don't fall into the trap of using so many that your text becomes heavily abbreviated.

Another form of abbreviation is using initials for people's names (WH Auden, TS Eliot). The old-fashioned style would write these names as W.H. Auden and T.S. Eliot which is a hangover from typesetting. You will still see spaces after initials in many academic publications but the more concise style (without full stops/periods) is growing in popularity elsewhere.

▶ Try not to use too many abbreviations in a document; any more than two or three a page, review what you have written.
▶ If you do have to use abbreviations, make sure they appear consistently, e.g. BBC, not B.B.C as well.
▶ Consider using an alternative, rather than the abbreviation, e.g. 'computer memory' rather than 'RAM'.
▶ Avoid unintentional repetition, such as 'PIN number'; 'PIN' stands for 'personal identification number'.

Capitalization

You should not stop using capital letters completely – just avoid sprinkling your prose with a capital every time you write an Important Letter. Capitals should only be used for:

▶ proper nouns, such as Africa, Caitlin, Harrods
▶ at the beginning of a sentence, e.g. 'Once upon a time...'
▶ in titles, e.g. 'the Lord Mayor'; 'I'm studying at the University of Kent'.

Double negative

In many languages, doubling (or even tripling in some cases) the negative serves to add emphasis to the meaning. In English, the understanding is that two negatives equal a positive. So using a double negative can confuse your reader. Does 'We didn't do nothing' mean 'We did do something' or 'We did not do anything'?

If you find you have written a sentence that has more than one of the following in it, you are guilty of a double negative and confusing your reader:

▶ Nothing
▶ Never
▶ None
▶ Nobody
▶ No
▶ Nowhere
▶ No one.

A double negative that does not immediately look like one is 'cannot help but': 'not' and 'but' are both negatives so do not put them both in the same phrase – use one or the other. Double negatives can also occur in sentences that use verbs with negative meanings; this makes them harder to spot.

▶ I cannot doubt that this is difficult.

Double negatives can be useful if you want to add a subtle meaning to your sentence: 'I would not say that I don't agree with the decision' is a more delicate way of saying 'I don't think the decision was the right one'. Other useful – and polite – double negatives:

▶ It is not bad.
▶ You are not unattractive.

Apostrophe

In 2001, a former journalist, John Richards, set up the Apostrophe Protection Society (www.apostrophe.org.uk). He thought he would get a few like-minded people to join; within a month, over 500 people had got in touch from around the world and the numbers continue to grow. There is now also a Friends of the Apostrophe in Australia and Apostrophen-Katastrophen in Germany.

We touched on the apostrophe in Chapter 2. It is worth mentioning again because it does seem to be the bane of some people's lives, particularly where *its* and *it's* are concerned. The two are quite different:

- ▶ With an apostrophe – it's = it is, it has (this is a 'contraction').
- ▶ Without an apostrophe – its = a possessive word (the cat licked its fur).

Remember: No possessive pronoun ever has an apostrophe.

If you are unsure whether to use an apostrophe for 'its' or not, check if 'it is' sounds right in the sentence (the cat licked *it is* fur = No, wrong). If substituting 'it is' doesn't fit or does not make sense, then use 'its' without an apostrophe.

There are some words that look like they should have an apostrophe but don't need one. For example: 'three months pregnant' is a descriptive phrase; it is not modifying anything or acting as a possessive so there is no need to have an apostrophe.

THE APOSTROPHE AND SINGLE WORDS THAT END IN 'S, X OR Z'

Advice on this can differ from style book to style book about whether words ending in s, x or z should have just an apostrophe or an apostrophe s/x/z (*Chris's* car or *Chris'* car'; *Dickens's* novels or *Dickens'* novels – they are all grammatically correct).

So which style should you use? Some words sound better with just the apostrophe (*Euripedes'* plays' is preferable to '*Euripedes's* plays; *Mrs Bridges'* recipes as opposed to *Mrs Bridges's* recipes – just say them out loud and you can *hear* that there are too many s and z sounds with the second versions) while others (the *fox's* cubs) are just fine with the apostrophe s. It is up to you whether you use the second 's' or not.

The good news is that it is a matter of style and preference. There is a tendency to just have the apostrophe without the extra 's' because it saves space and looks cleaner on the page.

Did you know?
In older English, it was common to add -es to a word to show possession (Charles – Charleses). Over time, people dropped the -es (from speech and writing) and just left the 's', with an apostrophe to show the possessive form.

Insight
'Off of' is just wrong. You get off something, never 'off of'. The 'of' is redundant ('She got off the bus' – not 'she got off of the bus').

Ellipsis

As we saw in Chapter 2, an ellipsis describes when certain words are missed out of a sentence or phrase.

You can show an ellipsis using the punctuation mark (three dots – no more, no less).

▶ It must be clear what words are missing from the sentence, otherwise you can confuse your reader. For example: 'We ate the meal with relish' – does that mean with appreciation or with pickles?

▶ If you do leave out words, you must be careful not to change the meaning of the original statement.

'An' before 'h'

It used to be acceptable to write 'an hotel', 'an heroic effort' and so on. Nowadays, we don't speak like that and it is no longer necessary to write like it either. The reason it came about was that the words were originally French and the 'h' was not pronounced so you needed the consonant 'n' to make things clear.

Who – whom

The pronoun, 'whom', seems to be slowly disappearing from English (certainly spoken English) because there is such uncertainty over when it should be used. 'Whom' is being replaced by 'who'.

The rule, however, is straightforward:

▶ **Who** – use for the subject (Who is shouting? =' who' is the subject of the verb)
▶ **Whom** – use for the object (I'm not sure whom to ask ='whom' is the direct object of the verb).

Who/whom should match similar subject and object pronouns:

▶ **Who** – he, she, we, they
▶ **Whom** – him, her, us, them

'Whom' may cause writers problems but it has not yet disappeared from use. As it is still with us, it is a good idea to use it correctly. As Bill Bryson says in his book *Troublesome Words*:

There is, in my view, a certain elegance in seeing a tricky whom properly applied.

Plagiarism

…otherwise known as copying someone else's work. When you borrow words, ideas or text from someone else, you acknowledge their contribution. Taking words without such an acknowledgement is plagiarism – stealing, in other words.

If you quote from another book or use anyone else's material, you may need to seek permission to use it. If you use substantial amounts of somebody else's material while it is still in copyright (i.e. during the life of the author plus 70 years after their death), you must get the author's permission and, possibly, pay a fee for its use. If you only use a *small* amount of material this should be covered by the 'fair usage' principle, as long as you fully credit the source of the material. The amount of copy deemed to be 'fair usage' depends on the length of the original material, and five to ten per cent is a good guideline as to the limits; as such, you could quote a bit more from a novel than you could from a poem or song.

▶ It is even easier to cut and paste great chunks of text from the internet. Some people do not seem to consider this plagiarism, but it is.
▶ If you use other people's work, either get permission from them to use it or keep a list of all the sources so you can credit them clearly.
▶ Open forums and blogs are easily accessible so be careful what you write on them if you want to use them in your work; they can be copied by others.
▶ If you think you might have written something that sounds familiar (and belongs to someone else) by mistake, type it into a search engine and see if that takes you to the source.

Be warned, there are several free online tools that allow people to check whether a work has been plagiarized. They are particularly popular with teachers who can run their students' papers through the checker to see how much of it is all their own work. Around 98 per cent of universities in the UK use Turnitin, a computer programme that scans essays, matching text to a database of 155 million student papers, 110 million documents and 14 billion web pages. In 2010, around 3 million essays were checked using the programme. If you do use work from another source, always remember to accredit it correctly; these facts, for example, were taken from an article on the BBC website (*Plagiarism: the Ctrl+C, Ctrl+V boom*, Tom Geoghegan, BBC News Magazine, 2 March 2011).

And plagiarism can have serious consequences. Original ideas and text are covered by copyright law. If you steal someone's work, you can be prosecuted for copyright infringement or sued in court for loss of earnings and reputation.

Plagiarism includes:

▶ not putting quotes in quotation marks
▶ not giving accurate information about where the quotation comes from
▶ taking someone else's written words and not crediting them
▶ copying so many words that they make up most of your work.

To credit someone else, you need to give enough information so that your reader, if they wish, can go and find the source. You need to give at least:

▶ the author's name
▶ title of the work
▶ name of the publisher
▶ date of publication
▶ academic works may include page references as well.

Wordiness – padding and fillers

Wordiness, or verbosity, does not add anything useful to a text. Strip a passage of verbal padding and you do not lose the meaning; if anything, you gain clarity. All writers are guilty of being wordy and long-winded at times. Why do we do it?

▶ We are frightened of leaving something important out.
▶ We write as we think and therefore wander off the point.
▶ It is easier to write more than less.

We talked about the length of sentences and the advantages of brevity in Chapter 3. Wordy, long-winded sentences should be avoided. Introductory phrases ('As a matter of fact', 'By and large',

'For the most part') really play no important part in a sentence; they are the written equivalent of clearing your throat before getting to the 'proper' sentence. Even 'There are...' and 'There is...' can be discarded without losing the sense of the sentence:

▶ **There are** many men who suffer from hair loss in later life.
▶ Many men suffer from hair loss in later life.

Not only do you get a shorter sharper sentence but you lose the woolly start and go straight in with a strong noun and verb. Stick to the point. It has its advantages. Daniel Oppenheimer (Princeton University) wrote a research paper, 'Consequences of Erudite Vernacular Utilized Irrespective of Necessity: Problems with Using Long Words Needlessly', which showed that the simpler you write, the cleverer readers think you are (*Applied Cognitive Psychology 20: 139-156*. Published online 31 October 2005 in Wiley InterScience, www.interscience.wiley.com).

Tell-tale wordy phrases that don't really mean anything and which should be avoided:

In my opinion	In a manner of speaking
All things being equal	As I understand it
It goes without saying	To all intents and purposes
As of right now	Under these circumstances
May or may not be	To the best of my recollection

If you do a plan (discussed in Chapter 4), you will think first and then write; rather than try to do them at the same time. Summarize first; tell people why you are writing this piece, then give them the supporting facts.

Wordiness	Brevity
ensure	make sure
give an indication	show
particulars	details
per annum	a year
prior to	before
purchase	buy
terminate	end
additional	extra
afford an opportunity	allow

Wordiness	Brevity
as of the date of	from
at this moment in time	now
as a consequence of	because
acquaint yourself with	read
as you may or may not know	as you may know
apart from the fact that	but, except
came to an agreement	agreed
commence	start
comply with	keep to
consequently	so
costs the sum of	costs
due to the fact	because
during which time	while
having regard to	about, for
few in number	few
for the purpose of	to
in addition to	besides
for the reason that	because
subsequent to	after
in respect of	for, about
on the grounds that	because
prior to	before
start off	start
in excess of	more than
in order to	to
in the course of	during

Keeping it simple

Writing does not need complicated language, long words and technical terms to get its meaning across. Its purpose is to inform, educate or entertain (and sometimes all three of those things at the same time). As a writer, you can achieve that by keeping your writing clear, simple and straightforward.

This chapter has been about what *not* to do. In the next few chapters, we will look at writing for different occasions and in different media.

10 THINGS TO TRY

1 Practise summarizing and cutting down. Take a newspaper story of several paragraphs long and try to summarize it in 20 words.

2 Look for clichés in books, newspaper and magazines. Replace them with plain English; does that make the meaning better or worse?

3 Write a list of well-used clichés and try to reinvent some alternatives.

4 Draw up a list of the words you misspell frequently, then set up your computer to AutoCorrect those words.

5 Keep a list of any acronyms and abbreviations that you come across. Do they work in their shortened form or should the writer have written them out in full?

6 Find sentences that use modifying adverbs, like 'only' and 'just'. Move them around the sentence to see how they change the meaning.

7 Look for examples of tautology when you are reading. Remove the surplus words and see if that improves the piece.

8 Check your writing for examples of redundant words; are there any phrases that you use a lot? Edit them out of your work.

9 Look for nominalizations. Change them to verbs and adjectives. How does that affect the writing?

10 Familiarize yourself with American English and British English spellings; make sure you stick to one style or the other and don't mix them.

6

Business writing

In this chapter you will learn:
- *how to avoid business jargon*
- *how best to use the active and passive voice*
- *the difference between being personal or impersonal*
- *how to write different business documents.*

> *If language is not correct, then what is said is not what is meant; if what is said is not what is meant, then what ought to be done remains undone.*

Confucius

This chapter is about 'business writing' – a catch-all description to cover the writing that people do at work (with the exception of journalism or any creative writing). So, for the purposes of this book, business writing can cover writing reports or memos for government departments and charities, writing as a private individual (such as minutes for your sports club) or as an employee (a marketing plan for the sales team, a presentation for the Board, for example and so on); it is not just confined to commercial companies.

We talked about formal and informal styles already in the book; in other words, the difference between a chatty, conversational writing style used between friends and a more professional, business-like style. Business writing is a type of formal writing but it has moved away from the rigidly old-fashioned style of 'Thanking you in anticipation…' and become more relaxed and natural, much closer to a way of speaking in fact. However, being 'relaxed' and 'natural' does not mean sloppy grammar and poor spelling.

A 2004 survey by the National Center on the Evaluation of Quality in the Workplace found that American employers regarded communication as the second most important job skill ('attitude' was considered the most important).

▶ Busy people want to understand and grasp what you are trying to say quickly.
▶ Good clear communication gives a positive, professional impression of you and/or your company.
▶ Communicating clearly makes things happen; work gets done, projects get finished.

The paperless office may have been achieved by some organizations, but the majority of us still have desks, drawers and shelves full of written documents. Computers, far from relegating paper to history, make printing off (and reprinting) our work extremely easy. Memos, reports, proposals, strategy documents, appraisals...we are writing more than ever. In the old days, managers would rely on their secretaries to produce written documents; now everybody is able (and often expected) to type a memo, write a letter, send an email, or produce a report themselves. Your work needs to stand out from all this printed 'noise'.

▶ Write and produce a document only if it is necessary.
▶ Make the document brief and to the point.

The ability to convert an idea into words that people can read and understand is central to many people's work. Even though your job description may not state that 'writing' as a part of the role, it will be a crucial part of your job. As such, it is a craft and therefore can be learnt and improved upon.

> *It's impossible to calculate the ultimate cost in lost productivity because people have to read things two and three times.*

Mike Huckabee, Vice Chairman of the National Governor's Association and Governor of Arkansas, commenting on a National Commission on Writing report, 2005

Education and academia has always had writing at the heart of the learning process. Essays, dissertations and presentations are an expected part of schooling. In business, written documents aimed at potential clients are extremely important in getting new business. But being able to communicate effectively with colleagues (presenting new ideas, data, strategies and plans) is also part of business and productivity. Communicating by written word is crucially important.

Many business documents are routine and are often done automatically with very little thought. Whatever the document, you should always give some thought and consideration to what you are writing.

- ▶ Why are you writing it in the first place?
- ▶ What do you want to achieve?
- ▶ What response or action do you require?

Insight

In business, aim for a simple, straightforward writing style. Simplicity suggests honesty and conviction. Long-winded, wordy text suggests you have something to hide. If you would not *say* it yourself, don't write it.

'Officialese'

We covered jargon, gobbledygook and waffle in Chapter 5 but it bears repeating when talking about business writing. What many organizations have in common is an inability to communicate in clear, concise English. 'Officialese' and 'bureaucratese' are just two of the names for it. Here is just one example: in 2011, Bedfordshire and Hertfordshire police forces issued a joint press release about changes to firearms licensing reviews. It was 351 words long, full of corporate-speak and took two or three paragraphs to get to the point. The following is an excerpt from the press release:

> *With a view to carrying out this function in the most effective and efficient way possible, the proposals include the withdrawal of routine home visits to people renewing their licences, an approach which has already been adopted by a number of forces across the country. The new approach will see the introduction of a risk-assessed process where enhanced intelligence checks will identify those who should receive a home visit. In addition a programme of random visits to licence holders will be introduced without waiting for the expiry of their current licence.*

The Essex Police force, also issued a statement about the same changes to the fire arms licensing reviews:

We are moving towards renewal notices by post rather than the current practice of making personal visits. The move is currently under consultation.

It is hard to understand why people use such language when they write because it is surely self-defeating to write business English in a complicated and jargon-filled way. As the Plain English Campaign points out, the main advantages of plain English are:

▶ It is faster to write.
▶ It is faster to read.
▶ You get your message across more often, more easily and in a friendlier manner.

All of which should be an advantage when trying to communicate with your readership (and your customers). If a document looks hard to read or is difficult to understand, your readers are not going to want to work their way through it. Some of them may have no choice; if it is a work-related document, they may have to read it – but they won't necessarily understand it or enjoy reading it.

▶ Jargon is very easy to skim through and ignore; if your readers are doing that, they can easily miss the message you are trying to get over.
▶ Make your text as straightforward and clear as possible.

The following phrases often appear in business writing; the clearer, alternative phrase appear in the second column.

Typical business writing	Clearer alternative
Should you require further clarification, please do not hesitate to contact us	You can call us on…
We refer to your letter of 23 February	Thank you for your letter of 23 February
The team will perform an analysis of	The team will analyse…
We will facilitate a meeting with the sales team	We will organize a meeting with the sales team
Can we make a recommendation that	We recommend…
As per our conversation	As we discussed…

Typical business writing	Clearer alternative
We respectfully acknowledge receipt of	Thank you…
In accordance with your wishes	As you requested…
Confidential in nature	Confidential

We must have a better word than 'prefabricated'. Why not 'ready made'?

Winston Churchill

Jargon can be an effective specialist language, used within an industry or discipline, that acts as a useful shorthand – but only when all parties know what is being said. Business language, especially in technologies such computing, automotive and electronics, is getting increasingly specialized – and with that comes a lot of new words and phrases.

- ▶ Is it jargon or acceptable specialist language? Always think of your audience.
- ▶ Will they understand the terminology?
- ▶ Do you want them to understand the terminology?
- ▶ Or do you want them on the back foot, unsure of your meaning…so that you can claim you meant something quite different later on?

If you have to use jargon, it is often worth explaining what it means. That way you come over as helpful and understanding, rather than a show-off who cannot write clearly.

Some words and phrases to avoid:

- ▶ Aforementioned
- ▶ Notwithstanding
- ▶ Prior to
- ▶ Hereby
- ▶ In accordance with
- ▶ At the present time.

For a bit of fun, you can go to the Plain English website which has a gobbledygook generator (www.plainenglish.co.uk/examples/gobbledygook-generator.html). Click on the button and a random piece of business jargon will appear. At the time of writing, a couple of random clicks on the button produced:

We need to get on-message about our knowledge-based reciprocal paradigm shifts.

I can make a window to discuss your interactive organizational resources.

Being honest and open

Long, rambling sentences appear far too often in business writing, especially bureaucratic documents which can strangle all meaning. In fact, it can sometimes appear that organizations are being deliberately unclear in order to hide something – especially when things go wrong. It can be tempting to wrap the facts up in a lot of vague clichéd phrases. The more obscure you are, the less genuine the apology feels.

Tell people why you are writing. State your purpose clearly; if the reader knows fairly early on why and what you are writing, they are more likely to continue to the end and pick up what is important. The following apology from the CEO of Facebook, Mark Zuckerberg, is clear, concise and to the point. He holds his hands up and admits mistakes were made and apologizes. Nothing is hidden or wrapped up in waffle and jargon:

We really messed this one up. When we launched News Feed and Mini-Feed we were trying to provide you with a stream of information about your social world. Instead we did a bad job of explaining what the new features were and an even worse job of giving you control of them. I'd like to correct these errors now.

Mark Zuckerberg, Facebook blog, 2006

Active / passive

We previously discussed both active and passive voice in Chapter 1 and Chapter 4, paying particular attention to the advantages of using the active voice. The passive, though, can be particularly useful in business and report writing:

▶ It can create a distance between the writer and reader.
▶ It can give emphasis to a particular noun, e.g. 'Our company has been awarded top prize in the national awards'.
▶ It can emphasize the action rather than the actor, e.g. 'The woman was attacked and robbed'.

- It can be used when you want to be tactful, e.g. 'The computer files were wiped'.
- When you want to avoid taking the blame, e.g. 'Mistakes were made' instead of 'We made mistakes'.
- When you do not know how or what the actor/doer is, e.g. 'The candidates were picked from all the recent entrants'.

The downside of the passive voice is that it can:

- make writing long-winded and wordy
- be confusing
- be less active and dynamic.

When to avoid the passive (with suggested alternatives):

Passive	Active
Arrangements have been made	I have arranged
The meeting will be led by Alan Smith	Alan Smith will lead the meeting
Your complaint has been investigated	We have looked into your complaint

Verbs – imperative voice

The imperative form of the verb is the one used when giving orders, instructions or commands such as 'Sit down', 'Send me the information, 'Listen to the statements'.

Writers, especially when it comes to business writing, can be a bit timid about using the imperative. There seems to be a feeling that it comes across as rude or abrupt. But there is nothing wrong with it. The concise tone and implied 'must' (rather than 'should') is useful when writing manuals, cookbooks or giving instructions. The following are all imperatives:

- Create a hole in the template as indicated.
- Measure equal amounts of flour and sugar.
- Recognize the value of asking staff for their opinions.
- Shut the door behind you.

If you are worried that you are being a bit abrupt, you can always put 'please' in front of the command.

Plural or singular?

Should a company name be considered singular or plural? A company is a single unit; but it is also made up of individuals. Should Acme Inc. be known for 'its' innovative thinking or 'their' work-life balance?

In America, a company is usually treated as a collective noun, has a singular verb and singular pronoun. In Britain, a company is usually referred to in the plural. It is a matter of choice for the writer. Just be consistent throughout.

Putting conclusions first

The conclusion of a piece of writing often has the best bits in it. Why leave those until the end? There is a strong chance a lot of your readers will not have made it that far. At school and college, we are taught to structure our essays to have introductions, main body and conclusions. Outside of the classroom, not everyone has the time to read through right to the end. Journalists have to put the most interesting facts first, with the less important facts toward the end. Newspaper editors cut stories from the bottom up. So it is important to get the most interesting, relevant points in early on because that grabs your reader and holds their attention and that bit of the story is more likely to stay in rather than be edited out.

There is no reason, in business writing, why you cannot put your conclusions at the beginning. Or whichever points are going to be of the most interest to your readership. The rest of the document can explain and support your opening statements.

Tone of voice

If you are writing for your organization, the tone of your writing voice must match the culture or brand that you represent. You will no doubt have a good idea of how your business should come over but look at its mission statement for other clues about the company's values and how it sees itself. If it talks about being 'passionate' or 'committed' about what it does, is your writing reflecting that passion and commitment?

Always be courteous, even if you have to complain, criticize or chastise. There is no need to cause offence or be rude. Being courteous does not mean using old-fashioned expressions ('your kind consideration', 'your humble servant', 'your esteemed order'); it means showing consideration to your readers. If you write in a courteous tone:

▶ you will not offend your reader
▶ you can be turned down by someone without jeopardizing future business.

The aim is to be tactful and not cause offence. If someone writes to you in an offensive tone or annoys you, resist the temptation to reply in kind.

Generally, business writing is about clarity and rationality. The tone is usually rather neutral and fairly unexcitable. It is not necessarily the place for self-expression or personal emotion. However, that does not mean that you cannot show some personality. Just don't go over the top.

Insight

If you are not sure what tone to adopt, be guided by the tone of the people you are trying to communicate with. Copy their style and tone.

Personal or impersonal?

Even if you are writing on behalf of the company that has a reserved, formal feel to it, keep a human face. Use personal pronouns like 'you', 'we', even 'I'. Don't talk about people ('the applicant', 'the customer', 'the supplier') in the third person; you would not if they were sitting opposite you.

We will advise customers of their delivery	We will tell you when your order will be delivered
Further information is available from...	You can get more information from...
Suppliers should contact us...	You can contact us...

Calling your organization 'we' makes you, as a company, more approachable and genuine-sounding. This is true whether you are writing for an internal or external audience. Using 'we', rather than 'I', when writing to colleagues shows that you are aligning yourself to the values and objectives of the company, rather than making statements solely as an individual.

In academic writing opinion is divided about whether using 'I' and 'we' is suitable or not. Personal pronouns do not sit easily in scientific papers but work well when the writer is discussing personal opinions or judgements.

Insight

In his essay, 'The Philosophy of Punctuation', Paul Robinson complains that there is an epidemic of semicolons in academic writing. He feels they are being used in a lazy fashion, to 'gloss over an imprecise thought. They place two clauses in some kind of relation to one another but relieve the writer of saying exactly what that relation is.' If you are tempted to use a semicolon in your essay or report writing, make sure that you are not guilty of this charge. (*Opera, Sex, and Other Vital Matters* University of Chicago Press 2002)

Writing as part of a team

Business writing often involves writing as part of a team; you contribute your part (the sales projection), along with human resources, the estates team, the marketing department and the finance people. Alternatively, you might be the editor or part of the writing team that has to both write and edit other people's copy.

Everyone who is contributing to writing a document should have a clear idea of what the purpose of the document is. They should also understand exactly their role is in that writing team. If necessary:

▶ draw up a list of who is doing what
▶ write down each individual's responsibilities, the timescale and any procedures that need to be observed
▶ show what, if any, style guidelines need to be observed.

Internal documents

Whether they are memos, reports, briefs or emails, internal documents are often about protecting your back and presenting your side of the story. You cannot hide behind anonymity (as writers of external documents can); people know you and what you do. Be very clear about what you want to achieve from the document. Make sure your message is clear and unambiguous.

Keep your audience in mind when you write.

▶ Are you writing for your superiors? Managers, directors, Board level?
▶ Do you want something from them? If so, have you spelt it out clearly enough?
▶ Are you writing for your colleagues?
▶ Get your message over quickly and clearly. They don't have time to wade through long-winded unintelligible text.

Insight

If you want to communicate something that is private and confidential, think first about committing it to paper (or computer). Very little can be kept entirely confidential from people you would rather not know your business.

▶ What is the subject? Make that clear from the start.
▶ Let the reader know why you are writing to them.
▶ If there are problems, put things in a positive light.
▶ State your case clearly to your reader.
▶ Show the benefits.
▶ What response do you want? Let your reader know what you want them to do once they have read your document.
▶ Be concise; edit and revise to cut out unnecessary words, develop your main idea and keep the words flowing smoothly.

MINUTES

Minutes should accurately record what has happened (been discussed, agreed and 'actioned') at important meetings. They are a permanent record of what happened, explain what happened to people who were not there and can be used to settle discussions or disagreements at a later date.

The style of minutes can take one of three forms:

▶ Minutes of resolution – which record the main conclusions, but not the details of the discussion that took place.
▶ Minutes of narration – which summarize all discussions, the decisions made and the conclusions reached.
▶ Verbatim minutes – which are word for word; usually only used for court documents.

If you are responsible for recording the minutes, make sure you record the names of everyone present and any who sent apologies. Get yourself comfortable and use whatever method of recording suits you (writing down on a notepad in longhand; shorthand; using a recorder).

It is usually not necessary to record every word spoken (unless you are required to record the meeting verbatim) but minutes should include:

▶ the name of the organization
▶ the type of meeting (monthly board meeting, specially convened)
▶ date, time and place of the meeting
▶ names of people there, including who is chairing the meeting
▶ apologies – people who were unable to attend
▶ an opening statement that records whether the minutes of the previous meeting were approved or needed revision
▶ new business (record who made and seconded any motions)
▶ action – what is required, who is doing it and when
▶ date, time, place of the next meeting
▶ time the meeting was adjourned (not always necessary).

Insight

Always type up the minutes of a meeting as soon as you can. It is much easier to get a sense of what was discussed while the meeting is still fresh in your mind, rather than leave it until almost the next meeting, when your memory has faded and you can't make sense of your cryptic notes.

MEMOS

A memo is a written message from one person to another (or several others). Memos can provide or request information, inform of or request actions.

Printed memos are being replaced by emails nowadays. However, if you are still producing memos, you need to include the following:

- ▶ To – who you are writing to
- ▶ From – your name
- ▶ Ref – what is the subject matter?
- ▶ Date
- ▶ Opening and closing – you do not need a formal opening or closing (i.e. no salutation)
- ▶ Space for your signature.

REPORTS

A report collects and interprets data. It aims to:

- ▶ inform
- ▶ analyse
- ▶ motivate
- ▶ record
- ▶ persuade
- ▶ instruct or
- ▶ recommend

so decisions can be made and action taken.

This is an ordered, well presented form of data and the report itself needs to look polished and professional – whether it is to be read by colleagues, clients, superiors or outsiders. The report represents you and your company.

The report can be informal or formal, aimed at colleagues or external readers. If you are writing a formal report, add an abstract; this is a summary of the whole report, about 100–120 words long. It should be able to stand on its own. It is standard practice in academic writing to produce an abstract which can be listed in libraries or journals of abstracts.

Abstracts:

- ▶ cover the main points
- ▶ do not go into great detail
- ▶ are written in a non-technical language
- ▶ act as a preview to entice the reader to read the whole report
- ▶ can be used as hand-outs.

An annual report is aimed at a company's shareholders and should tell them how their company is doing. All too often, an annual report is seen as a marketing tool and can be full of jargon and banal clichés. Warren Buffet, in his Chairman's letter of 1983 to the shareholders of Berkshire Hathaway, did not hide behind vague phrases and clichéd words:

> **We will be candid in our reporting to you, emphasising the pluses and minuses important in appraising business value. Our guideline is to tell you the business facts that we would want to know if our positions were reversed. We owe you no less... We also believe candour benefits us as managers; the CEO who misleads others in public may eventually mislead himself in private.**
>
> Chairman's letter, Berkshire Hathaway, 1983

Taking time to present the report properly is not just for cosmetic effect. It helps the information contained in the report to be read and understood more easily. A well-presented report represents the data; a badly presented report does not inspire confidence in the data contained in it. If you cannot get your spellings right, it suggests, how can we trust your conclusions?

- ▶ Give some thought to the title; don't just call it 'Report'. Describe what the report is about.
- ▶ Have a table of contents; it divides the report into manageable and digestible sections.*
- ▶ The introduction should state what the report is about and why it has been written.
- ▶ The conclusion should describe the conclusions and how they were reached.
- ▶ Keep both introduction and conclusion as brief as possible.
- ▶ Use headings to summarize the argument and help divide the text on the page; make sure the headings are descriptive (not 'Point one', 'Point two').
- ▶ White space makes the report more inviting and easier to read.

*If the report is a short one, you will not need a table of contents. Use headlines to show a logical progression that guides the reader through the document.

If you are lucky (and it is well written, interesting and engaging), your readers will read the whole report. At the very least, they will read the introduction and the conclusion so make sure that you include the relevant, important points here so that they remember them. If nothing else, that can encourage the reader to go back and look at the whole report.

▶ Always print off a test copy of the report before you circulate it. It is easier to proofread from paper than from the screen.
▶ Double-check spelling and grammar, as well as your facts.
▶ What is the aim of the report? Has it achieved its aim?
▶ Who are the readers? Is the layout and language suitable for the intended audience?
▶ Use page numbers if the report contains more than two pages; they help guide the reader through to the end.
▶ Put the date and time (in the header or footer) so people know they are reading the most up-to-date version.
▶ Point size needs to be big enough to read in comfort.
▶ Use larger type size for titles and headings so they stand out.
▶ Don't go mad with the presentation. You do not need lots of colours, typefaces, images and special effects to make a report work. They can have the opposite effect, making it hard to read and understand.
▶ Don't mix typefaces; use a plain, unadorned style that is easy to read.
▶ Try to avoid a background image unless it is quite faint and the text stands out easily.

Insight

Everyone likes a story. Use story-telling techniques to keep your reader's interest. Case studies are a good example; they act like a mini-story.

PROPOSALS

Proposals are similar to reports but, while a report deals with information on what has happened in the past, a proposal looks to what might happen in the future.

A proposal is a plan to *do* something:

▶ Its aim is to persuade the reader to take a course of action.
▶ It can be one or two sentences or several pages long.
▶ It can be informal or formal.

Always make your proposal look professional. Whether long or short, formal or informal, a proposal should be written with the reader in mind. It should include:

- ▶ background information
- ▶ a description of the proposed plan
- ▶ a schedule, costs, additional factors
- ▶ a course of action
- ▶ qualifications, experience
- ▶ an emphasis on the benefits
- ▶ a summary.

PowerPoint

PowerPoint (or other slide presentation software programs) is used for several reasons:

- ▶ as a visual aid during a presentation
- ▶ as a hand-out after a presentation
- ▶ information for people who have missed the presentation.

The most common purpose, and the one that PowerPoint was designed for, is as a visual aid during presentation. It does not work as well as a hand-out given after the talk or if you have missed the live talk. That is because it is a *presenting* tool (and therefore a useful way of communicating with the audience), not an *explaining* tool. If you are intending to hand your presentation out afterwards, it might be worth considering doing so as a Word document and adding a bit more text. This will be more useful to the reader.

The most common content type for PowerPoint presentations is text. It can be in the form of lists, paragraphs, single words or phrases. How much text you use is quite crucial; poor presentations fall into two camps: those with too much text or too little.

Those with too much text tend to use PowerPoint as a sort of prompt, a script for everything that they want to say in person. At times, one feels it would be easier if they just handed over a printed version of their presentation and let you read it at your own pace.

At the opposite end, some people put the bare minimum on each screen. Competent and confident speakers can fill in the gaps that this minimalist approach creates. If the speaker is poor, however, this pared down style does nobody any favours.

When you are planning your presentation, establish who your audience is going to be:

- ▶ What do they know?
- ▶ What do they want to learn?
- ▶ What are their expectations?
- ▶ What do you want to achieve from this presentation?

Generally, your audience will not know how long your presentation will last or how long it is going to take. Resist the urge to produce pages of text, graphs, statistics and facts; plan the structure and order carefully.

- ▶ Start with a brief summary – explain what your presentation is going to cover.
- ▶ Clearly state the problem or situation that the presentation is going to address.
- ▶ Ensure the slides back up what you are saying; they are not the main focus of the presentation.

The text of the presentation must be clear enough to be read from the furthest point (or worst seat) in the room.

- ▶ Use between five and seven lines of text on each visual.
- ▶ Make an effort with headlines that grab the attention.
- ▶ Use upper and lower case in headlines.

Text is important in visuals but this can be enhanced with colours, layout and lists.

- ▶ Vertical bulleted pointed lists are popular in presentations and for presenting complex information. (See Chapter 3 for more information on lists). Although lists help people to scan key points quickly, try not to have the whole presentation as one long list of lists.
- ▶ Pictures or graphics can be useful when trying to convey complex arguments; they also help add interest to a boring visual.
- ▶ If using charts or tables, make sure the axes and data lines are clearly labelled.

When planning a presentation, there is a tendency to add more slides than you actually need. Resist the temptation to illustrate every single point with a separate slide. Keep it brief but not curt.

Insight

PowerPoint has collaborative tools so more than one person can work on a presentation. Errors will creep in if one person is not made responsible for proofreading/checking text so always nominate one person as the editor.

Do resist the temptation to add all the whistles and bells that PowerPoint contains. Known as 'PowerPointlessness' by some, it is the act of adding gadget-y transitions from one slide to another, including sounds and special effects that have no real purpose, benefit or use – other than showing off the fact that you know everything that PowerPoint has to offer.

Speeches

Mark Twain wrote that 'It usually takes me more than three weeks to prepare a good impromptu speech.' A good speech is planned carefully beforehand. A well-written talk can turn an indifferent speaker into a good one. If you have to give a presentation or speech, ask yourself:

▶ What is the topic?
▶ Who is the audience?
▶ What is my message?

The topic should be clear and straightforward; don't try to throw too many ideas into one speech because people will not be able to remember them. Knowing who your audience is will help you pitch your talk at the right level; are they knowledgeable about the topic or do you have to give a lot of background information? Remember what we discussed in Chapter 4: who are the primary readers (or listeners in this case) and who are the secondary? You should be able to write your key message as one sentence and keep referring back to it as you prepare your speech so that you don't stray off topic.

A good speech should have a memorable opening and closing. Techniques for opening and closing speeches:

▶ Ask a question.
▶ Use a quotation.
▶ Tell a story.
▶ Tell a joke.
▶ Give a statistic.

Insight

Take a leaf out of some of the great orators when writing a speech. Some of the most memorable speeches use word play like repetition, rhythm and alliteration (see Chapter 9 for more on word play).

His speeches left the impression of an army of pompous phrases moving over the landscape in search of an idea.

William McAdoo about President Warren Harding

Speeches are meant to be heard, not read. If you are writing a speech, bear this in mind. The more conversational in tone you make it, the easier it is to say it out loud. That means you can contract words (like 'can't', 'won't') and use short sentences, even sentence fragments. Once the speech is written, *always* read it out loud so you can hear how it sounds. If you stumble over some phrases, consider rewriting them so they are simpler to say.

You can get much more detailed information on effective speech writing from *Make a Great Speech* in the Teach Yourself series.

Did you know?

In 1863, Abraham Lincoln gave his famous Gettysburg Address. It followed a two-hour speech (13,607 words long) by the politician and educator, Edward Everett. The Gettysburg Address (272 words long) took two minutes. Lincoln's address is the one that went down in history as one of the greatest speeches. In this case, less was definitely more. It was easily understood, made an impact and was remembered, unlike the speech that went before.

Business plans

A business plan has been described as a company's CV or resume; it identifies your organization and what you aim to achieve. It is a plan for a new venture. Like any proposal, a business plan aims to persuade the reader. The reader can be from within the organization, a potential investor or the bank.

The plan should describe what the business is all about, the product or service it will provide, anticipate any problems, how they will be dealt with and the course of action to take in order to provide the product/service.

Depending on the audience, you may have to write several versions of a business plan; for example, the bank will be more interested in some details than a fellow executive would. The plan should include:

- ▶ **Mission statement** – see later for more information on mission statements.
- ▶ **Description of the business** – how it started and what it provides; keep it jargon-free.
- ▶ **Aims/goals** – where is it going; what is the plan for the future?
- ▶ **Analysis of the market** – show an understanding of the trends and characteristics of the industry; what is the anticipated growth in the market?
- ▶ **Marketing plan** – what actions will be taken for marketing and PR; how will they be tracked?
- ▶ **Financial analysis** – details of the company's financial status; strengths, weaknesses and potential growth.
- ▶ **Management team** – describe the abilities, experiences, skills of the key members.
- ▶ **Any supporting documents** – such as examples of promotional material, CVs of management team, inventory, price lists, copies of any legal agreements, etc.

There is no right or wrong length for a business plan; it depends on the type of business, the complexity of the business, who is to read the business plan and what the purpose of the plan is (is it for potential investors or employees, for example).

Insight

Organize your writing according to how your readers think about the subject. Put what they want to hear near the beginning of your document. For example, investors would want to know financial performance; new students would want to read about the history of the college/school.

MISSION STATEMENT

This summarizes what a company's vision is; its goals and purpose. While a mission statement is not confidential, it should be used as an internal document, rather than a marketing tool for the company brochure. It gives focus and meaning to the people who work in that company. It is also a document that should be reviewed as the organization grows and develops.

- ▶ It can be short (a few sentences) or several paragraphs long.
- ▶ It uses clear, straightforward phrases and sentences; not jargon.
- ▶ It should not be about how wonderful the company is but what it aims to achieve.

Tenders

Tenders are invitations by government bodies or organizations to suppliers of goods and services. 'Writing a tender' is how a supplier applies for a contract. Ninety per cent of all tenders submitted by organizations will include the following phrases:

▶ We are passionate...
▶ We believe...
▶ We are committed...
▶ We aim to...
▶ We are working towards...
▶ We are the leading company...

These are all subjective phrases that do not contain anything concrete or definite. Imagine how the readers of these tenders feel when they see the same phrases repeated over and over again. The purchasers are not looking for vague phrases; they want to see:

▶ We are...
▶ We do...
▶ We deliver...
▶ We operate...

When answering the questions posed in the tender documents, get to the point and be brief.

▶ Use bullet points where you can.
▶ Use sub-headings if a question covers more than one topic.

Sales material

This is often the first point of contact potential customers have with a business. First impressions count. Content and quality are key to giving that good impression. Don't let yourself or your company down by sloppy grammar and poor quality control.

A company brochure tells people what the organization is all about: where it has come from and what it has to offer. It can sometimes be a bit bland because it has to speak to a very wide audience, so has to be all things to all people.

See *Improve your Copywriting* (part of the Teach Yourself series) for more information on writing powerful and persuasive marketing copy.

Questionnaires and forms

Questionnaires should be easy to read, understand and fill in – ideally with as little effort on the part of the person filling in the questionnaire. Make them difficult, labour-intensive or confusing and you reduce the chance of getting people to respond.

You can ask different sort of questions to get a response:

▶ Yes/no questions – easy to answer (e.g. 'Would you order from us again?' Yes / No').

▶ Multiple-choice questions – to get more detailed answers (e.g. 'Is your house: Terrace / Bungalow / Detached / Semi-detached / Flat / Maisonette').

▶ Questions that rate the answer in a sliding scale (e.g. 'Did you find the experience: Excellent / Very good / Good / Fair / Poor / Very disappointing').

OPEN OR CLOSED QUESTIONS

All the above examples are closed-ended questions; the question is answered but you cannot expand or explain your answers. Open-ended questions allow people to answer more fully. For example: 'Tell us what you liked about the welcome you received when you arrived?' allows the respondent to recount their experience and give their views in their own words. Open-ended questions usually begin with: how, why, tell me about…

Open-ended questions require a bit more thought and effort from the person filling in the questionnaire so they can deter people from responding (because of the extra thought and effort involved). Have a mix of closed and open-ended questions to encourage people to respond.

- ▶ Keep questionnaires as short as possible; if they are too long, people won't fill them in.
- ▶ Explain that the answers will ultimately benefit the customers (or clients, students, patients – whoever you are asking questions of).
- ▶ The questions should be clear and straightforward so people know what information is needed.
- ▶ Group subjects together.
- ▶ Put the easy questions at the beginning.
- ▶ Leave space so people can leave extra comments if they want to.
- ▶ Give clear instructions on where to send the questionnaire when it has been filled in.

Make sure you leave enough space for people to write their information. Partially sighted people tend to have larger handwriting than most so you need widely spaced lines or large boxes. It is law in many countries that you have to meet the needs of your blind and partially-sighted customers. There are, for example, 2 million people in the UK with sight problems; they all need to be able to access, understand and use business literature.

Business letters

We look at letter writing in more detail in the next chapter but it is worth mentioning that business letters are acting as ambassadors for the company. They need to make a good first impression.

- ▶ Use good quality stationery.
- ▶ Ensure it is well-laid out (lines straight, printed clearly, well-spaced with margins).
- ▶ Use appropriate language and tone.
- ▶ Be clear and concise.
- ▶ Give clear instructions to the reader as to what action to take next.
- ▶ Put contact details (telephone, email, fax number) after your name if they are not included on the headed notepaper.

Footnotes

Footnotes appear frequently in academic writing but can be used elsewhere. Use sparingly; they should only appear if you really cannot fit something into the main body of the text but is still important enough to be included in the report or essay.

Style guide

If your organization does not have a style guide, it might be worth considering putting one together. It is common practice in magazines, newspapers and other businesses. It helps writers within that organization keep to the 'house style'.

You can add anything that you think is important. The guide does not have to be a large document. It can give people pointers on what to use and how to present any written work produced within the company, such as:

- ▶ correct typeface
- ▶ point size
- ▶ formatting
- ▶ spellings
- ▶ punctuation
- ▶ general recommendations (i.e. are abbreviations or contractions allowed?).

The advantage of a style guide is that it gives a uniformity and consistency to documents. Rather like adding the logo to literature, the website, uniforms and so on, it gives the impression of order and consistency within a professional organization.

School work

School and academic work is another type of formal writing. *Write Great Essays and Dissertations*, from the Teach Yourself series, gives more detailed, practical advice on assessed written work, whether at school, college, university or postgraduate level. However, we will look at personal statements here.

The majority of colleges and universities, both in the UK and the US, require a personal statement from each student. These are especially useful for the college if they do not interview potential students face-to-face. An application form gives a student's grades and references. If everyone who is applying for a popular course has wonderful grades and glowing references, the only thing that will make them stand out is their personal statement.

Your personal statement needs to show:

- ▶ what you want to study and why
- ▶ that you are reliable, conscientious, hardworking
- ▶ you can cope with the pressures of the course
- ▶ any relevant interests, skills, hobbies, gap year experience
- ▶ enthusiasm, commitment, passion.

Avoid:

- ▶ making jokes
- ▶ making political statements
- ▶ making spelling and grammatical mistakes
- ▶ starting every sentence with 'I'
- ▶ showing off and exaggeration
- ▶ plagiarism; there are ways of checking if you have copied another statement
- ▶ using famous quotations; they want to hear your voice not someone else's
- ▶ using an 'academic' vocabulary that you think will impress
- ▶ telling lies.

Look at the prospectuses for the college/university course that you want to study to find out what they are looking for. You need to show those qualities in your statement.

You should write as if you were addressing interested and intelligent friends of your parents. A strong opening statement will help make you stand out from all the others. You want to get your reader's attention so they look through your statement. Finish with a strong last sentence to make it memorable. 'Strong' statements do not mean wacky, over-the-top or outrageous. Clear, precise and enthusiastic makes more sense and is more appealing to the reader.

A personal statement is not a letter so do not include 'Dear Sir or Madam' or 'Thank you for reading this'. Write it in an essay style. Remember this is a statement about you and what you want to study, rather than an essay purely on the subject of the course itself. Make sure you include the following:

- ▶ **Introduction** – why you want to do the course, your enthusiasm for the subject
- ▶ **Current studies** – how they will help with the degree course
- ▶ **Any relevant work experience** (this is for vocational degrees, like law, teaching or medicine)
- ▶ **Skills and personal qualities**
- ▶ **Hobbies, gap year experience** – relevant to the course and to studying at university
- ▶ **Conclusion** – why the college should take you.

You will not get it written in one go; be prepared to write several drafts before you are happy with it. Many personal statements have to be submitted online so you need to get it right before hitting the 'send' button. Write out your drafts in a Word document before committing it to the online application. If you are sending it online, remember that you will be unable to use bold, italic and underline.

Personal statements differ slightly from country to country so always check with the admissions board of the college, state or country to see what is required. For example, UCAS, in the UK, allows you to enter 4,000 characters (which includes spaces) or 47 lines of text (including blank text), whichever comes first.

Did you know?

Copying a friend's brilliant personal statement is not a good idea; you will be found out. In the UK, for example, UCAS use a Similarity Detection Service which checks all personal statements for any similarities. Any statement that shows a similarity of ten per cent of more is reviewed. The applicant and the universities/colleges are contacted if the similarities are confirmed. It is then up to the admissions tutors to decide if any action should be taken.

The language of business

The pace of business life is fast; turnaround is expected to happen quickly. Writing well and effectively under these conditions can be challenging. Despite speed and new technologies, old habits die hard and there are still some worn out phrases being used in formal business writing

('The above mentioned...', 'Reference your letter of...', 'Thanking you in anticipation...'). These out-dated, wordy phrases do nothing for the clarity and conciseness of a document.

English is a global language, used as the language of business, diplomacy and popular culture. There are more people who use English as a second language than there are native speakers of the language. If you do business abroad, it is extremely likely that you will be dealing with someone who has English as a second language. Whether they are fluent in English or only have a basic grasp of the language, it is important that you write clearly at all times.

Good writing cannot improve a bad idea. What it can do is show the idea up for what it is.

▶ Choose the form of communication carefully.
▶ Present the document so it looks good (clear layout), gives an impression of efficiency and reliability – it should be easy to read, neat and structured so flow is logical and coherent.
▶ Check your facts carefully.
▶ Use simple, straightforward expressions; avoid jargon unless you are absolutely sure of your audience.
▶ Keep the sentences short if you are giving instructions or directions.

10 THINGS TO TRY

1 Look at how different brands address their readers. Notice the difference between formal and informal. What works and doesn't? What impression of the company do you get from the language?

2 Look for examples of business-speak and see if you can make the copy flow by substituting shorter, simpler words.

3 Make a list of all the jargon associated with your job or subject. Which ones would an outsider understand and which ones need explanation? Come up with a list of alternative words.

4 When planning a presentation see if you can cut the number of slides by one third and still get your message across.

5 Find something that you wrote recently, how did you plan it? Was there anything you could have changed while you were drafting it so that it was easier to write?

6 Review business letters and reports. Circle any examples of the passive voice. Would it sound better if it used the active voice?

7 Look for uses of the imperative. Which examples work? Which ones need to be more concise? Do any come across as rude or abrupt? What would make the tone better?

8 Read newspaper articles; see how they put the most important facts in the first paragraph. Can you do this with your business writing?

9 Find a report or something similar. Move the conclusion to the beginning of the report. Does this improve it?

10 Devise a style guide for your organization (or yourself as an individual).

7

Letter writing

In this chapter you will learn:
- *how to plan a letter*
- *when handwritten is best*
- *how to write different types of letters, including CVs*
- *about having the right materials to hand.*

> *I have only made this [letter] longer, because I have not had the time to make it shorter.*
>
> Blaise Pascal, 1657

Despite the advent of the telephone and all other forms of electronic communication, letters still play an important part in our lives. While a telephone call or text can get immediate results, a letter allows you to think things through, plan what you want to say and work out what kind of response you want to get.

A letter also shows that you have made the effort, whether typed or handwritten. You have gathered the stationery together, written the letter, addressed the envelope and posted it. It is tangible. It can be exciting or touching to receive. It is written with the recipient in mind. It is individual.

In formal writing, social rules dictate how we address certain people. You will find the correct way to address people (heads of government, members of the church, the armed forces, etc.) in books of etiquette or websites such as Debretts (www.debretts.com) or Emily Post (www.emilypost.com).

Informal letters, such as those written to family and friends, have very few rules but you still want to be able to get your news across clearly, without ambiguity or bad grammar. Business letters are more formal. If you are writing of behalf of the organization that employs you, remember that you are representing that company at all times, including when you write a letter.

Planning your letter

A letter is a permanent record so you make sure you plan it carefully.

- ▶ What points do you want to make?
- ▶ What is the most logical order to put the points in?
- ▶ What are the facts?
- ▶ What are your opinions?
- ▶ Do you want something to happen as a result of writing the letter? If so, have you made that clear?

Write out a rough draft first. You can see if the points follow logically, whether the letter makes sense and if you need to add or delete anything. If you have typed the first draft, print it off and proofread it from a hard copy; that is how your recipient will read the letter and it is easier to spot mistakes this way.

When you are happy with the letter, print or write it out; put it in the envelope, which should have the full and correct address, and then post it.

SETTING OUT

The majority of letters have a beginning, middle and end. In other words, you open a letter with at least a date and greeting (or salutation), follow it with the main body of the letter and close with a final sentence and ending (your name).

Date

It is now more usual and acceptable to write the date as 2 February 2011 and not 2nd February 2011. Avoid using abbreviated dates (for example, 3/9/2012) because it can be confusing; some countries start with the month, others with the day (see Chapter 5).

Punctuation

You no longer need to add commas and full stops after:

- ▶ each line of the address
- ▶ the greeting
- ▶ the ending line.

For example: Mr P Robinson (not Mr. P. Robinson). Normal rules of punctuation apply in the main body of the letter.

Greeting/salutation

If you know the reader well enough and are on first name terms with them, use their name in your greeting ('Dear Alex'); otherwise use 'Dear Mr Brown'. If you are writing to a woman and are not sure what title she prefers to use, write 'Dear Ms Jones'. If you do not know the name of the person you are writing to, use 'Dear Sir' or 'Dear Sir or Madam'.

Headings

If you want to use a heading to refer to the subject of your letter (for example, 'Postal delivery times'), put it on a separate line after the greeting, in bold. You don't need to write 'Re:', nor do you need to put the heading in capital letters. Not every letter needs a heading so don't feel you must add one to every letter; it is entirely up to you.

You don't normally need sub-headings in a letter unless it is a long one; in which case, headings can break up your subject matter into more easily read chunks of text.

Endings

Just have a simple one-liner to close your letter that is relevant to the message. If you want a response or some kind of action to follow once the person has received your letter, then say so ('A prompt reply would be appreciated' or 'I look forward to writing to you again'). Vague closings ('I look forward to hearing from you soon') do not mean anything and are unlikely to prompt the reader to act.

If you are writing a formal letter and have used a person's name at the beginning of the letter, use 'Yours sincerely'. If you have had to use 'Dear Sir or Madam', use 'Yours faithfully'. If your letter is to someone you know well, you can choose a more informal ending ('Yours truly', 'Best wishes', 'Lots of love' and so on).

Signature

Even if you have printed your letter, you should sign it by hand. This makes it more personal. If you are producing hundreds (or thousands) of letters, get an image of your signature (a jpg, for example) to put here or use a font that looks like a handwritten signature.

P.S.

'Post scriptum' is Latin for 'after writing' and is used when you have got something to add after you have finished the letter. In the days of typewriters and hand-written letters, it was more common to see a P.S. Nowadays, using a computer, it is easy to go back and insert something that you may have forgotten. You can still use a P.S in an informal letter (it can be hand-written or typed) and it can be particularly useful in a direct marketing letter where it gives you the chance to reinforce your sales message; it should not be used in a formal business letter.

Contact details
If you have printed letterheads for personal or business use, your contact details (address, phone number, email and possibly website) will already be on the page. If not, you should write your address and the date on the top right hand corner of the first page.

Layout

Your address*
Townsville
ABC 123

[Leave a line between the address and the date]

Recipient's name and address
Somewhere else
XYZ 456

Dear Mr Smith

Leave a line after the greeting and start the first paragraph of the letter. You can indent the first line of each paragraph if you wish. That is up to you. It can be a useful visual break if you do not leave a line in between subsequent paragraphs.

If you do leave a line between paragraphs, it is not necessary to indent the first line. If you do indent the first paragraph, make sure you are consistent through the letter and indent each subsequent paragraph too.

When you come to the end of the letter. Finish it off with the simple, clear and straightforward one-liner as discussed above before signing off the letter.

Yours sincerely

[put your signature here]

Type your name underneath – useful if your writing is illegible and your signature is hard to read.

*In the UK, the sender's address is right aligned. In the US, it is often left aligned.

ALSO

▶ **Date** – you can also position the date on the left hand side of the letter, before or after the recipient's address. Always write the month as a word.

▶ **Reference** – if writing a business letter, you can add a reference number, which can help to identify the correspondence and make filing easier. The reference can either be put after 'Dear...' on a separate line and before the opening line of the letter or before 'Dear...'.

▶ **Signature** – if you think the recipient may not know whether you are male or female, you can put your title ('Mr', 'Miss') in brackets after your name.

▶ **pp** – indicates that you are signing the letter on behalf of somebody else because they are not there to sign it themselves (pp is Latin and stands for 'per procurationem').

▶ You do not need to type out your address if you are using printed letterheads which already have the name and address on them.

▶ **Enc** – stands for 'enclosures' and you should add at the bottom of the letter (under your signature and typed name) if you have added another document other than the letter itself. Type 'encs' if there is more than one additional document.

▶ **Cc** – add after 'enc', along with the name of the person/s, if you are sending them a copy of the letter.

▶ If you are writing to a friend, you don't need to add their address.

▶ If you are writing a business letter, make sure you put a contact number (phone and/or email) underneath your name so the recipient knows how to contact you.

If you are writing a formal or business letter and you find that your letter does go onto a second or possibly third or fourth page, make sure you add a page number. You can also put a date and the addressee's name, if you wish, on the following pages. There is no need to add anything at the foot of the previous page (such as 'continued'); if there is no closing sentence and signature, it shows that the letter continues onto another page.

> Always use a new page rather than printing onto the back of the first page.

Try to start a new page with a new paragraph. Make sure you have at least three or four lines of the letter, plus your closing section ('Yours faithfully', etc.) on the following page.

Insight

It is not always clear what the sex of the writer may be; either because they have a name that could belong to a man or a woman (Lesley, Chris, Kim, Lee, Terry, Sam) or it is a foreign name, unfamiliar to the reader. If you are writing to someone and you do not know whether they are a man or a woman, use their full name ('Dear Kim Robinson').

Wordiness

A fairly constant theme throughout the book has been to warn against wordiness; 'keep to the point', 'be concise' and 'brevity is a good thing'. For the most part, this is true; there are, however, times when it pays to add a bit of padding to your opening sentences, usually when you have to write something unpleasant, such as breaking bad news. 'Dear Sarah, Joe died yesterday...' is a bit blunt and gets to the point almost too quickly. 'Dear Sarah, I thought I should write to you to let you know that Joe died yesterday...' is a gentler lead in to what is obviously going to be a difficult letter, both for writer and reader.

Otherwise, avoid clichéd, wordy expressions. Here are some examples.

Avoid	Preferred
As per our conversation	As we discussed
Attached herewith	I have attached
Awaiting your reply, I remain	Yours sincerely
Please don't hesitate to call me	Please call me
Per your request	As you requested
Pursuant to our conversation	As we discussed
We are in receipt of	We have received

Handwritten letters

A handwritten letter, especially in this age of computers, looks like you have made an extra bit of effort. Traditionally, people write certain letters (such as condolence and love letters) rather than print them off. However, if your writing is dreadful, it makes sense to type and then print your letter, rather than confuse and exasperate your reader with pages of illegible scrawl.

A good compromise is to write the greeting/salutation ('Dear Victoria') and the close ('With best wishes') by hand and type the main bit of the letter.

If you think your handwriting needs help, look at '*Improve your handwriting*' (from the Teach Yourself series) which can help you correct problems and develop a mature and individual style.

Writing a letter of complaint

This is a formal letter, so lay it out as if writing a business letter. When complaining, you should try to remain courteous and polite. Even if you are angry, there is no need to be rude and give offence. If you want to get a problem solved, it is easier to do so in a positive way, rather than a negative one.

While it may feel awkward, complaining is actually easier when you do it face-to-face because you can soften your words with body language. It is harder to strike the right note of complaint and courtesy when writing. Phrases to avoid:

▶ I must insist…
▶ It is not our/my fault…
▶ You/they failed to…

Always write your letter of complaint to a named person, rather than an anonymous executive or customer service department. You may have to make a phone call to find out the right person to address the letter to but it is worth it to make sure it lands on someone's desk. This way, it is easier for you to follow-up if needed and harder for the named individual to ignore.

If you are writing a letter of complaint:

▶ Write as soon as possible; don't leave it too long because your complaint will be harder to investigate.
▶ Be as brief as possible. Your letter is more likely to be read and dealt with if it is fairly short.
▶ Don't be rude; it will not help your cause.

- Remember that the fault may not lie with this person and that they may be able to help you.
- In the opening paragraph, explain what the issue is (why you are writing).
- Describe the details (for example, the item bought, when and where and what was wrong with it; the service received or not received). Keep to the facts; write them down clearly and concisely and avoid getting emotional.
- In the second paragraph, explain what you would like done to resolve the situation (a refund, a replacement, an apology).
- Finally, thank the recipient for their time.
- Always send copies of documents or receipts with your letter, not the originals.
- Make sure you have included your telephone number and/or email address, as well as your address, so you can be contacted easily.
- Keep a copy of your letter of complaint; keep a copy of all other letters (both sent and received).
- Send it special delivery if you want to be sure that it arrives safely.

If you have to deal with or respond to a letter of complaint, most of these points apply as well.

- Keep calm; there is no need to be rude.
- Respond immediately; even if it is just a letter of acknowledgement stating that you are looking into the complaint and will write again with a full response within a set period.
- Keep a copy of your letter and send it special delivery to make sure it arrives.

USEFUL WORDS

acceptable	accurate
attention	aware
complain	compromise
damage	defect
dissatisfied	error
experience	fault
grievance	guarantee

inaccurate	incident
mistake	negotiate
oversight	reasonable
replacement	resolve
responsible	restore
satisfy	settle

USEFUL PHRASES

▶ Bring this matter to your attention...
▶ I am sure you will want to correct...
▶ I was inconvenienced...
▶ I want to register my dissatisfaction with...
▶ I noticed an error...
▶ I am confident we can resolve this situation...
▶ Please check your records...
▶ Uncharacteristic error...
▶ By writing, I hope that this will not happen again...

Apologies

If you are replying to a letter of complaint or something similar, be professional not emotional. However upset the person making the complaint is, you must be as polite and helpful as possible.

If you are going to apologize, write the letter promptly and say that you want to apologize as soon as possible in your letter; don't wait until you are nearing the end. If the fault is yours or your company's, acknowledge the fact. Even if it is not your fault, try to keep a positive note in the letter by stressing what you can do for the other person, rather than what you cannot.

▶ Write the letter sooner rather than later.
▶ Depending on who you are writing to, you can use an informal (for a friend) or a business format.
▶ Start with an apology and take responsibility for your actions (especially if writing to a friend).
▶ Explain what went wrong (if writing formally) and say what you are going to do to rectify the situation.
▶ Close the letter with an apology.

accept	acknowledge
admit	apologise
committed	failed
fault	mistake
repair	responsible
restore	thoughtless

USEFUL PHRASES

- ▶ I admit…
- ▶ I/we are responsible…
- ▶ Please accept my/our apology…
- ▶ There is no excuse for such…
- ▶ We will certainly correct the error…
- ▶ May I take this opportunity to set things right?
- ▶ I/we will correct this by…
- ▶ In order to correct the situation…
- ▶ Yes, you are correct…

I have the words already. What I am seeking is the perfect order of words in the sentence. You can see for yourself how many different ways they might be arranged.

James Joyce

Thanks

No matter how effusive you are in a verbal thank you, nothing can replace a written note or letter of thanks. Everyone appreciates a 'thank you' letter.

- ▶ They can be short, conversational and friendly.
- ▶ Send your thanks sooner rather than later.
- ▶ You can write a thank you on anything (notepaper, a card, postcard).
- ▶ A handwritten note is more thoughtful than one that is printed.
- ▶ A note or letter shows more thought (and effort) than an email.

USEFUL WORDS

cherish	useful
enjoyed	delighted

generous	excited
lovely	kindness
perfect	overjoyed
satisfied	remember
thanks/thank you	stunning
thrilled	touched
treat	unforgettable

USEFUL PHRASES

▶ delightful choice
▶ extraordinary treat
▶ generous gift
▶ I will always be grateful/thankful for...
▶ keepsake to treasure...
▶ perfect choice/timing
▶ thrilled to receive
▶ what a kind/lovely/thoughtful thing to do...
▶ you made my day

Love letters

Do people still write love letters? We hope so. Always write a love letter by hand. Handwritten letters, whatever the subject or intent, add a personal touch and show that you have taken the time and made the effort to put pen to paper.

▶ Write down a rough first draft; when you are happy with the content, you can write it out carefully.
▶ Be sincere and write from your heart.
▶ Use some nice stationery, rather than plain white paper.
▶ Start with 'Dear...' (or something more intimate if the relationship is an established one) and close with something affectionate.
▶ Don't close the letter with 'Yours sincerely'.
▶ You do not have to observe the formality of your address, the recipient's address; just the date will be fine.
▶ Never write in haste. Leave it a day (or at least a few hours) before you post it so that you can be sure you are happy with what you have written.

adored	amazing
beautiful	close/closeness
dreams	generosity
perfect	precious
respect	thoughtfulness
share	understanding

USEFUL PHRASES

- ▶ my own
- ▶ perfect in every way
- ▶ you are an exceptional person
- ▶ I am so lucky
- ▶ you listen to me
- ▶ you complete me
- ▶ missing you
- ▶ very special
- ▶ always thinking of you
- ▶ you make me a very happy man/woman
- ▶ I love you

Invitations

If the invitation is to colleagues, peers or customers:

- ▶ Keep a professional tone throughout.
- ▶ Introduce yourself and/or the company if necessary.
- ▶ Include the date, time and location of the event.
- ▶ Explain what the purpose of the event is (the launch of a new product, for example); include any information on dress code, what to bring and so on if necessary.
- ▶ Say that you look forward to seeing the guest at the event.

If you want to invite friends to an event but choose not to use a traditional invitation (such as the engraved copperplate 'Mr & Mrs Neil Smith request the pleasure of your company...' style), you can write them a letter. The advantage of writing an invitation letter means that you can add additional information (such as set the tone for the event, share memories and so on). You can sign off the letter with a more informal finish ('Best wishes', 'lots of love', etc.).

RSVP

If you are inviting someone to an event, you want to know whether they will come or not. Putting 'RSVP' (which stands for *respondez s'il vous plait* – French for 'please respond') on an invitation means the invited person must indicate whether they will attend or not. Some invitations have 'RSVP, regrets only' which means the invitee should only reply if they are unable to attend. If you receive an invitation (with RSVP or not on it), it is polite to let them know if you are going to turn up.

When writing your acceptance, be guided by the tone of the invitation. If it is a formal invite, write a formal reply (even if you know the people really well) and vice versa. If the invitation was hand-written, it is polite to respond in kind.

USEFUL WORDS

announce	attention
attend	celebrate
company	enjoy
greet	inform
join	joy
meet	pleasure
reply	request

USEFUL PHRASES

- ▶ We really hope you will be able to come and celebrate with us...
- ▶ Happy to announce...
- ▶ Please join us...
- ▶ We want to introduce the new...
- ▶ This is your special invitation to...
- ▶ Please say you will come.
- ▶ Your presence will make the celebration complete.
- ▶ It will be wonderful to get together and catch up.

Congratulations

The style of this kind of letter is conversational and friendly; write as if you are talking to someone. If you are writing a personal letter of congratulations, a hand-written letter always looks good, especially if your handwriting is legible (if it isn't, type it). If you are writing to a business associate, a typed letter on headed paper is appropriate.

▶ Use the world 'congratulations' early on in the letter.
▶ State the reason for your congratulations at the start of the letter ('Congratulations on the birth of your son').
▶ Show your enthusiasm.
▶ The letter should just be about your congratulations; don't add anything else.
▶ Keep it short and sweet.

USEFUL WORDS

accomplishment	achievement
admire	celebrate
compliment	congratulate
dedicate	enterprising
excellent	exceptional
exciting	extraordinary
happy	impressive
inspiring	meaningful
memorable	milestone
momentous	outstanding
proud	sensational
superb	talent/talented
thrilling/thrilled	tremendous
well-earned	

USEFUL PHRASES

▶ Congratulate you on...
▶ Delighted to hear of your...
▶ You deserve...
▶ It was great to hear about...
▶ I want to offer you my warmest/heartiest congratulations.
▶ It is a well-deserved honour/recognition...
▶ Wish you every happiness...
▶ It is an outstanding achievement.

No-one will enjoy reading what you have not enjoyed writing.

Philip Larkin (quoted by Kingsley Amis, *The King's English*)

Get well

Many of us, when we hear that someone is ill, will send them a card ('Get Well Soon'). However, if that person is in hospital or house-bound, a chatty letter, full of news and gossip, is much more welcome. You do not have to go on about their illness, just entertain them and take their mind off things.

USEFUL WORDS

cheer/cheerful	encourage
heal	healthy
hope	rapid
recovery	recuperate
support	

USEFUL PHRASES

▶ Best of health
▶ Completely well again
▶ In our thoughts and/or prayers
▶ Time to heal
▶ Thinking about you
▶ I feel certain you will be...
▶ I was so sorry to hear about...

Condolences and sympathy

Letters of condolence and sympathy are not just sent when someone dies; they can be written when someone has lost a job, suffered a divorce or breakdown of a relationship, a business has failed – any occasion, in fact, where you want to let someone know that you are thinking of them at a bad time.

These are difficult letters to write and people feel awkward about what to say and how to say it. But do write something rather than avoid doing anything. The recipient will be grateful that you have made the effort.

A letter is much more thoughtful than a card. You do not have to write a long letter; you can be brief but remember to be kind.

Traditionally, letters of condolence are handwritten; it shows that you have made a special effort. If you are writing to a business associate, typed is fine as well. If you think you can give advice that will be helpful, then do so. Offering help is always appreciated even if you are not taken up on your offer. If you do say you will help, make sure you mean it.

▶ Write immediately, as soon as you hear the news.
▶ Start the letter with a clear, straightforward statement of sympathy, stating why you are writing, e.g. 'I was so sorry to hear of your...'.
▶ Use your relationship with the recipient to guide the tone of the letter; are you friends or acquaintances? If you are not a close friend or relative, introduce yourself at the beginning of the letter, e.g. 'I worked with your husband in his last job'.
▶ Try to avoid being overly sentimental or show pity.
▶ Focus the letter on the recipient, not on how you feel.
▶ Don't use harsh words like 'death', 'sacked', 'dumped'.
▶ Don't use clichés.
▶ Never say you know how they feel; grief and unhappiness are very personal feelings, unique to each person.
▶ If the letter is about someone who has died, use an appropriate memory or anecdote about them. Describe the qualities you liked about them.
▶ Offer help; be specific if you can, e.g. 'I'll drop a casserole round at the weekend for you and the family'.
▶ Finish on a warm, hopeful note.

When you have written your letter, put it to one side for a while and then go back and re-read it to check that you have got the tone right before you send it.

USEFUL WORDS

affection	bereavement
care	comfort
consolation	concern
difficult	grief
gift	healing
hope	loss
mourn	overcome
sad/saddened	sympathy

- ▶ A loss for all who knew him
- ▶ I know you have had your difficulties
- ▶ Extend my/our sympathies
- ▶ You are in our thoughts and/or prayers
- ▶ My/our hearts go out to you
- ▶ Saddened to learn
- ▶ So sorry for your loss
- ▶ Will always be remembered/be missed
- ▶ Will always have fond memories of
- ▶ Is there anything I/we can do for you?
- ▶ You have my love and friendship

Newsletters

Some people send out a round-robin newsletter at Christmas or other annual holidays, letting people know what the family members have been up to in the past year. Communities (like sports clubs) use them to keep in touch with each other. Businesses also use newsletters to let customers, employees and colleagues know of important information and developments.

FAMILY NEWSLETTERS

- ▶ Work out a plan: are you going to work through the year chronologically? By person or by topic?
- ▶ Try to keep it fairly short.
- ▶ Don't boast but be chatty and informative.
- ▶ Be aware of who you are sending the newsletter to; if someone has not had a great year (lost their job, a member of the family, money is tight), they will not necessarily want to hear your glowing news so you may have to do a bit of editing for individual recipients.
- ▶ If you have printed the newsletter, add a handwritten message to each recipient.

BUSINESS / COMMUNITY NEWSLETTER

Newsletters are a useful marketing tool. They keep customers informed of new developments and let the employees know what is going on and give praise where it is due. You may choose to have one newsletter for both employees and customers or you can tailor each newsletter for a particular audience.

Adding information like charitable events, employee achievements (running a marathon, an unusual hobby), any sponsorship that the company has done to other stories about sales figures, new products, new directions makes it a more interesting read and less of a 'sell, sell, sell' document. It is a chance to promote a more human side of the company.

▶ Use a journalistic style of writing.
▶ Keep articles short.
▶ Mix up the subject matter (informal, entertaining, informative).
▶ Add images, photos and colour if possible.
▶ Use white space; it makes the copy easier to read.

Sales letters

Your aim is to persuade the reader to buy what you are selling, whether that is goods or services. You want your reader to be intrigued, charmed, surprised and rewarded. If they are, they are more likely to remember your sales message and do something about it.

When you write a personal letter, you use your own voice and style; when you write a sales letter, you have to use a tone and style that you know the reader will identify with immediately. So, writing a direct mail letter aimed at 20- to 30-year-olds would have a different style and vocabulary from a letter about travel insurance to the over 60s.

A sales letter needs:

▶ an opening headline or statement – grab the reader's attention
▶ a description of the produce/service and why it is useful or needed
▶ a closing statement that prompts the reader into action.

Sales letters should:

▶ be short (one page) and to the point
▶ have fairly short sentences
▶ be friendly
▶ address the needs of the reader (use 'you' rather than 'we')
▶ tell the reader the facts; they want to know how they will benefit

- ▶ give clear instructions on what to do next
- ▶ make it easy for them to respond; if it involves too much effort, people just won't bother.

For more information on sales letters and copywriting in general, look at the book *Improve Your Copywriting* from the Teach Yourself series.

USEFUL WORDS

changed	completed
created	demonstrate
increased	launched
reduced	reorganized
revamped	saved
succeeded	transformed

Job application covering letter

An application letter is another form of sales letter; you just happen to be selling yourself. These letters are all about you so don't be afraid to use the personal pronoun, 'I', a lot. Remember that the aim of the letter is to get you an interview, not the job. Show your ambition and enthusiasm. You want to get the reader interested in you and meeting you face to face. So it is all about showing your personality and qualities.

- ▶ Strike a friendly but not familiar tone.
- ▶ Be neat and present the letter so it is easy and clear to read; make sure it is clean (no stains or marks).
- ▶ Unless you are specifically asked to handwrite the letter, always type it.
- ▶ Refer to the position you are applying for at the start of the letter and say where you heard about the vacancy.
- ▶ Explain why you are interested in working for the company and why you want to be considered for this particular job (what are your strengths, skills, education, qualifications, experience).
- ▶ Keep it as short as possible; don't duplicate what is in your CV in the covering letter.
- ▶ To close the letter, indicate your availability for interview, thank them for their consideration. Finish with a sentence that shows your interest in the job.

A lot of writers are guilty of generalizing and being rather vague. This can be particularly true when writing job application letters: 'I am a good communicator with great people skills'. Look at that phrase again; it does not tell the reader much. Where is the 'for example' to support the statement? Back up comments like this with some concrete information.

Increasingly, employers are finding that fewer applicants are able to write clearly, grammatically and concisely. Make sure your letter has no errors and gives a clear message.

Insight

Always tailor your letter to each individual company. It is tempting to come up with a single generic cover letter that you can use for every job application but using a letter like this will reduce your chances of getting an interview. Prospective employers notice when you have made the extra effort.

Letter of enquiry

This is a way of approaching a company speculatively. They have not advertised a vacancy but you are writing to see if there are any openings. Include the following in no more than four paragraphs:

▶ Introduce yourself briefly and say why you are writing.
▶ Explain what you are looking for and where you heard about the company.
▶ What is it that interests you about their company? Explain why they may be interested in seeing you.
▶ Mention your qualifications and background briefly; refer to your CV, which you will have attached to the letter.
▶ Always thank them. Indicate when you would be available for an interview if they want to see you.
▶ Ask that they consider you if any vacancies become available.
▶ The tone should be optimistic, not begging.

USEFUL WORDS

accomplished	achieved
adapt/ed	addressed
adjusted	analysed
anticipated	available
balanced	completed

conducted	created
develop/ed	demonstrate/d
expand	establish
favourable	improve
increase	introduce
prepared	produced
problem-solving	propose
represent	restructured
specialize	strengthen

▶ I believe my experience as [give example] demonstrate the skills you are looking for...

▶ As you will see from my CV, my [selling, marketing, etc.] skills can add value to the position of...

▶ I have a solid background in...

▶ I now feel I am ready for a position of greater responsibility...

▶ I worked very hard to...

▶ I believe I am uniquely qualified/prepared for this position because [give example]

▶ I would like the opportunity to discuss this position with you...

▶ I look forward to discussing my ideas/proposals with you...

▶ I can make myself available for interview at [give availability]

CVs

A CV (curriculum vitae – Latin for 'the course of one's life') or resume gives a brief description of your personal details, work history and education. It is also the first impression (along with your covering letter) a prospective employer gets of you so it needs to be well presented. If your CV is full of spelling errors, grammatically incorrect and poorly laid out, it reflects badly on you.

Get that Job with the Right CV, also in the Teach Yourself series, goes into greater detail on how to produce a winning CV but we will look at the basics here. You need to make your CV stand out from the others – for all the right reasons. Avoid wacky coloured paper, peculiar fonts (stick to Arial or Times) and no smiley faces!

- ▶ Ideally take no more than two pages.
- ▶ Use 12 or 14 pt size so it is easy to read.
- ▶ Use good quality paper.

PERSONAL DETAILS

Make sure you include your:

- ▶ name, address, contact number (daytime, evening, mobile) and email address
- ▶ date of birth and age at time of application.

EDUCATION AND QUALIFICATIONS

Start with the most recent and work back. You can go all the way back to secondary/high school but don't if that is so long ago as not to be relevant to the current application. Use your judgement.

WORK EXPERIENCE

Start with your most recent/current job and work backwards. You need to include the year the jobs started and finished, who you worked for, your job title and what your role involved. Use short sentences to describe what you did and keep things positive.

FURTHER INFORMATION

This section can include skills and qualifications. It is not an opportunity to boast; keep it relevant to the job (for example, competent in computer programs such as Microsoft Office or a clean driving licence if the job involves driving).

HOBBIES AND INTERESTS

This section gives an idea of your personality and what you enjoy when you are not working. You don't have to come up with anything out of the ordinary. Use plain, straightforward English, keep sentences short and to the point.

REFEREES

You will need the names and addresses of two people who will provide references for you. Make sure that you ask their permission to include them on your CV. One is usually from either your current employer or is a professional person who you have worked with. The second can be someone you have known for a long time (a teacher, your doctor, priest, etc.). Referees should not be related to you.

Letter of resignation

Once you are sure that you wish to leave your current job, you should write a hard-copy resignation letter. Use the formal business letter format.

▶ Briefly state why you are leaving (going to another job, moving away from the area, etc.).
▶ Explain when you are leaving; you probably have the notice period written into your employment contract.
▶ Thank them for the time they have employed you.
▶ Keep the tone positive. You may have to ask them for references or deal with them in a business context in the future.
▶ If you think the reason for your leaving may upset them (they are a dreadful company to work for), you don't have to give that explanation. You can just state that you are leaving to pursue new challenges.
▶ If you enjoyed working for the company, then say so.

USEFUL WORDS

appreciate	benefited
developed	enjoyed
grown	opportunities
resign	support
thank you	valuable

USEFUL PHRASES

▶ I have benefited from my time here
▶ I have gained valuable experience
▶ Enjoyed working with the team
▶ It has been an excellent learning experience
▶ I have gained valuable new skills
▶ Seek new challenges/career direction
▶ I am most grateful/thankful for the opportunities you gave me
▶ I am sad to have to end this working relationship

General tips

PHRASES TO AVOID (ESPECIALLY IN BUSINESS LETTERS)

Business letters written 15 or 20 years ago would have been much more formal than those we write and receive today. What used to be acceptable is now dated; you could even offend the person you are writing to if you are too formal.

- ▶ I must inform you that...
- ▶ It has come to my attention
- ▶ Please be advised that...
- ▶ Thanking you in anticipation
- ▶ Kindest regards
- ▶ With reference to your letter

Insight

If you are writing to someone in another country, remember that humour and jargon do not always travel well and can be misunderstood. Be clear about time zones when you refer to times; use international measurements; and only use someone's first name if you know them well.

PROOFREAD

Always check through your letter when you have finished it. It is often easiest to print the letter off and read it from the printed page – that is how the recipient will read it. As well as checking for typos, punctuation and grammar, make sure you:

- ▶ have made the points that you wanted to
- ▶ have answered any questions that had been asked
- ▶ have been clear and concise.

Don't staple the pages together because they can tear the letter and staples can get caught on fingers and fingernails.

ADDRESSING THE ENVELOPE

Put your name and return address on the upper-left hand corner of the front of the envelope. The stamp (or franking) goes in the upper-right corner. In the middle centre, you put the recipient's address.

- ▶ Print or write all the information on the envelope before you put the letter inside.

- ▶ If you are writing to a friend and the envelope is too small to have two addresses on the front, you can add your return address on the back of the envelope.
- ▶ If you are sending the letter abroad, put the country it is destined for on the last line of the address. Use capital letters for the country.
- ▶ Put any instructions (Confidential, Please forward, Personal) on the left hand side of the envelope, below the return address.

STATIONERY

Always have stationery (including cards and postcards) to hand for writing letters, whether you are at home or work, including a supply of envelopes and stamps.

Business stationery should:

- ▶ be of good quality
- ▶ reflect the personality of the company
- ▶ have a logo or graphic
- ▶ include contact details, including postal address, website, telephone numbers
- ▶ include a registered office or number (usually at the bottom of the headed paper).

Continuation sheets can be used for the second or subsequent pages of a letter. They do not need to have all the contact details; the logo is usually enough. A plain white sheet of paper will be fine if the company does not have continuation sheets.

Insight

It is always useful to have a handful of cards, postcards and attractive stationery for informal communication. That way, you have something appropriate to hand and you won't be caught out. Look out for pretty cards and notelets at sale time.

10 THINGS TO TRY

1 Practise writing a letter of condolence; imagine a colleague has lost their mother. What would you write?

2 Study junk/direct mail letters; what catches your eye and why? What works well?

3 Write a letter of appreciation to a business that has shown you good service recently.

4 Find a formal letter that is more than one page; can you edit it down to one page without losing any of the information?

5 Study the letters page in the local paper. Write them a letter on a local subject you feel strongly about.

6 Write a chatty letter to a friend you haven't spoken to in ages.

7 Have a look at your CV and give it a makeover. Or, if your CV is up-to-date, offer to revamp a friend's CV.

8 Write a letter by hand. Is it presentable? Does your handwriting need smartening up?

9 Get different samples of writing paper. What would be suitable for business? What could you use for friends and family?

10 Write a piece for your company/club newsletter. Or plan to send one out to friends with your year's news.

8

··

Writing on the internet

In this chapter you will learn:
- *about writing emails*
- *about websites and the importance of keywords*
- *about blogging*
- *how to compose texts and tweets.*

> *I have come to believe that if anything will bring about the downfall of a company, or maybe even a country, it is blind copies of emails that should never have been sent in the first place.*
>
> Michael Eisner, former chairman of Disney

The arrival of the internet has transformed the way we communicate. With our PCs, laptops, notebooks and smart phones, we have almost continuous access to the internet. This is where we store information, contact friends and business associates, relax, play games and, of course, write. This chapter looks at all forms of electronic communication: from emails to tweets, websites and blogging.

Some sceptics have argued that the Internet is affecting our capacity for concentration and contemplation. The more people use the web, the argument goes, the less likely they are to be able to read and take in long and involved pieces of writing. We are certainly subjected to an almost continuous stream of communication. Does the constant bombardment mean that some of us tune out? If that is true, it can be harder to grab people's attention. An effective writing style is crucial if you want to keep your reader's interest and understanding.

Speed and informality sum up how the majority of us write in electronic communications. In many ways, how we write on the internet is closer to how we speak – and that is a good *and* a bad thing. Good because it encourages more people to put their thoughts down and they can do it easily. Bad because even though we can all publish our own work, there is very little editing on the internet.

Just a brief mention on the terms 'internet', and 'web'. Most of us use the two words interchangeably, even though they are two completely separate things. As long as you make your meaning clear, it is usually perfectly acceptable to use either word but just for information, the differences are:

▶ Internet – a network of computers that exchange information.
▶ Web – (Worldwide Web) made up of files that run on the internet.

> **Did you know?**
> People only really began to use the internet in 1993 when the National Centre for Supercomputing Applications released the Mosaic Web browser.

'Netiquette'

A word that derives from 'net' (internet) and 'etiquette' and means an acceptable and friendly form of behaviour when communicating online. Netiquette applies to chat rooms, emails and webpages. Basically, one should:

▶ be polite, particularly to people you have never dealt with before
▶ be brief; get to the point
▶ not shout (use CAPITAL letters); flame (write hostile, angry posts) or be a troll (deliberately upset people).

BOLD, ITALIC, UNDERLINING

Text read on screen is different from that on the printed page. Overuse of bold and italic is hard to read while underlining can be confused as an active link. The more you use these type styles for emphasis, the harder it is for the reader to work out just what is important.

▶ Combining bold and italic is the equivalent of shouting.
▶ Bold is useful in titles, to emphasize a word, to distinguish a command (such as 'Select' or 'Order here') and for warnings.
▶ Italics can emphasize a word or phrase, titles of books and films; you can use asterisks instead of italics in emails (plain text emails won't display italics).

When you use a computer, there is a wealth of weird and wonderful symbols and characters that are available to you. Anything from ✂ to ✉. Not all software can translate the special characters correctly so they are best avoided in emails and online. If you need to use them in a website, check with a designer that the software will support them. If something does not display properly, it can make the website look sloppy, badly-written and therefore not to be trusted.

Emails

The email is probably the most common form of written communication nowadays. Before, we would pick up the phone and make a call; nowadays, we are more likely to send an email. But while firing off a quick email to a friend with a few typing errors and dubious punctuation may be acceptable, it is not ideal for other recipients, particularly in a formal business context. Your friends know you; they will not necessarily be judging you on how your emails look. For other people, the first or only impression they get of you is from the email you send them.

ADVANTAGES OF EMAIL

- ▶ Quick and informal.
- ▶ One email can be sent to multiple recipients.
- ▶ It's cheap.
- ▶ A convenient way of communicating with people in different time zones.
- ▶ A variety of information, including video and pictures, can be attached and sent with an email.
- ▶ The recipient decides when to open and read it.

DISADVANTAGES OF EMAIL

- ▶ You can send and receive far too many emails.
- ▶ Junk mail can be a problem.
- ▶ Too informal at times.
- ▶ Too instant; it's easy to send something quickly and then wish you hadn't.
- ▶ Attachments can contain viruses which affect our computers.
- ▶ Confidentiality can be a problem.
- ▶ Can be a constant interruption throughout the day.

With the rise of smartphones, email looks as popular as ever. People can now access their emails at any time; they no longer need to be sitting in front of a computer. According to research less than 200 million people were using mobile devices to access email in 2009; that figure is predicted to grow to more than 1 billion by 2013. So, it is even more important to consider length and complexity when writing emails. Even with the most sophisticated smartphone, it is easier to read something short and to the point.

Insight

Writing short messages quickly but not clearly does have its pitfalls; they can lead to all sort of unfortunate misunderstandings, especially if the reader has been equally hurried in the way they scanned the email. You should be economical *and* precise.

The difference between a personal letter written at the beginning of the twentieth century and an email nowadays will be noticeable. The email will be shorter, chattier, more informal and immediate. This works well because people are more likely to scan an email, whereas they will read a letter (see 'Scanning' later). But even a short email has a beginning, a middle and an end. Take a moment to plan what you are going to write, no matter how short.

ADDRESSING YOUR EMAIL

'To' is for the person you are writing to; 'Cc' stands for 'courtesy copy' and is for people who need to see the email but not act on it; 'Bcc' means 'blind courtesy copy' so the addresses typed here are hidden from the other recipients. When using 'Cc' only copy people in if they really need to see the email, not just because you know them. Double-check that you have typed in the correct email address, especially if numbers as well as letters are involved; it is easy to confuse a '1' for an 'l', for instance. Unless there is a specific hierarchy within an organization that requires you to list people in the 'To' and 'Cc' boxes in order of importance, it is easier to list people in alphabetical order.

SUBJECT LINE

This is the first part of your message that the recipient sees. Give some thought to the subject line; summarize the message clearly and briefly. Some people receive hundreds of emails a day. Make yours stand out by actually telling them what the message contains. They are more likely to read it first if they know what it is about. 'Urgent',

'Help me out' or 'Reply' tells them nothing; while 'Julia – reply by 5pm please' or 'Information needed – not urgent' are much clearer. A good subject line draws the attention and helps with filing the email.

▶ Keep the subject line short so it is easy to scan; around 50 characters (including spaces) is ideal.
▶ Write as if it is a (short) sentence, rather than a title; this is easier to scan and looks more approachable and less formal. Start with a capital letter.
▶ Double check your spelling; a mistake will be the first thing your recipient sees.
▶ Remember that the recipient sees the 'From' line and the Subject line; they read them together to make sure that the email is not spam or junk mail.
▶ Avoid using all upper case, symbols for money (£ or $) and words such as 'buy', 'free', 'win', 'low rates', 'bad credit' which can all trigger spam filters.
▶ When you reply, the email programme automatically inserts 'Re:' (from the Latin 'about, concerning'). If there are several replies, it is easy to lose the sense of what the email is about and even have a subject line that does not relate to the main email. Make sure the subject line relates to the subject of the email.
▶ Never leave the subject line blank; it is rude.
▶ If your email message is going to be long, it can be a good idea to add [Long] to the subject line to prepare your reader.

Insight

If you know the person well enough, it is possible to conduct an email conversation using only the subject line and with no need to write in the text box. It is a great time saver. Don't do this with people you don't know because it can seem a bit curt and rude.

SUBJECT MATTER

Try to keep to one subject per email and get to the subject quickly. Don't bury your subject matter in waffle. It is easier for the recipient to deal with one thing, than work their way through several. A one subject email is also easier to file.

Tell your recipient:

▶ why you are writing to them
▶ what you expect them to do (or not to do)
▶ when you expect them to respond.

GREETING

Always include a greeting, whether it is 'Dear Mr X...' or 'Hello, Jim'. It shows that the email is for the recipient, rather than one of the people who have been copied in on the email. Should you start your email with 'Dear...', 'Hi...' or nothing at all? It all depends on who you are writing to. If you are sending a business email or writing to someone you don't know very well, politeness does no harm; so 'Dear' would not go amiss, neither would 'Hello'. However, writing 'hi' (or 'hey', 'yo' or something equally informal) to someone you have never met can irritate them before they have even begun to read the email. Err on the side of courtesy if you are not sure. If you do not know someone's name and you can't find out what it is, use their title, e.g. 'Dear Sales Manager', 'Dear Editor'.

USE PLAIN TEXT

Plain text is preferable to HTML (which creates webpage-style emails that have images) so that everyone can see and read your email as you intended. Images may brighten your email up and give it a bit more impact but many people's browsers (including mobile browsers) will not display images.

FORMATTING

Email programmes come with a default font setting, usually set at 12 pt, which is perfectly acceptable. Break the text into paragraphs rather than have one long block of copy. It is easier to read, especially on screen. Headings and words highlighted in bold help highlight important points. Leave the background white (easier to read the text) and don't play around with colours (which can be difficult for people who are colour-blind).

SUPERSCRIPT AND SUBSCRIPT

It is difficult to display either in email format. For superscript, it is acceptable to use the ^ symbol (found on the '6' key); for example, if you wanted to write $x + y = mc^2$, you can write x + y = mc^2. It is not possible to show subscript in an email so, for H_2O, you would have to write H2O.

BE CONCISE

If you receive a lot of emails every day you know how difficult it is to work your way through them. Short sentences and paragraphs are more likely to be read. Try not to write more than five paragraphs. If your message is longer than that, send it as an attachment with a covering email. Get to the point. A lot of us are guilty of starting our emails (and letters) with 'I thought I'd drop you a line... ' or 'I just wanted to let you know... '. Those phrases are unnecessary padding. So drop them. The only time when it is a good idea to have a bit of padding in your sentence is when you have to say something unpleasant, such as breaking bad news (see Chapter 7, 'Letter writing').

BULLET POINTS AND LISTS

Bullet lists are a good way to present information quickly and concisely. When scanning a page of text, lists help the reader remember the key points. They can make the layout look good too.

CLOSING

'Yours faithfully' or 'Yours sincerely' do seem too formal for the world of email. Nevertheless, you need some kind of sign-off; a phrase that lets the reader know they have come to the end of the message but that is not so peculiar or outlandish that they forget what they have just read and fixate on the ending. Even with business emails, you are safe with 'Best wishes', 'Regards', or 'Best'. Only put 'xxx' if you would kiss someone hello or goodbye if you met them face to face.

Avoid abbreviating your sign-offs (BR = best regards, BW = best wishes) unless you are writing to close friends.

ATTACHMENTS

If you are sending photos, try to keep them under 5Mb (easier for your recipient to download) and double-check you have added any attachments before hitting 'Send'.

EDIT AND REVIEW

Check that you have made all the points you wanted to. If you want some action or response, is that clear? Check for spellings and punctuation. A sloppy email shows that you don't really care and couldn't be bothered to check things before sending; not a great impression to give someone.

If you are angry, don't send an email for at least one hour (in fact, 24 hours is better).

Flaming should be avoided. Once you have calmed down, you can then write the email. Write what you would be happy and comfortable saying to someone's face.

REPLY PROMPTLY

Try to deal with emails as soon as possible. It is polite and shows the sender that you consider their email important. That does not mean you should be rushed into a reply; if necessary, you can let them know that you've received their message and are giving it your attention. Don't reply with one word answers, like 'Thanks' or 'OK'; they are not worth the effort to send or to read.

Insight

Try to get people to add your email to their contacts or address book; your emails will not end up in the junk mail folder.

TONE

In the early days of emailing, technology put some constraint on how – and how much – people wrote. The limitations meant that people had to be concise so abbreviations, acronyms and emoticons (which were formed using punctuation marks) became widespread. Nowadays, there is no need for these shortcuts but they still pop up from time to time; that is perfectly acceptable in emails to friends but less so in business and work emails.

If you are not sure how formal or informal to be when writing to someone, aim for a polite but conversational style at first. Be guided by the tone of their reply and match any subsequent emails to that.

There will be times when you need to be quite formal (when complaining, for example) so you should write as if you were sending a formal letter. Informal emails can be short, chatty and light on good grammar and punctuation; these are fine to send to friends. In the middle of the two styles is a more neutral tone; it is used in the majority of emails we send – at work, for business and so on. You can use contractions (can't, won't, shan't) and sentences can be short. The main aim is to be clear, concise and direct.

EMAIL ADDRESSES

When you set up an email account, take some time to think about what you are going to have as your email address. You could be using it for quite some time. At work, we rarely have a choice as to what we have as our email address; when it comes to personal addresses, what is funny or cute for a teenager may not be appropriate for an adult.

- ▶ You may have the moral high ground when complaining about poor service but you can weaken your argument if you have a daft email address. People do not take you seriously.
- ▶ Don't just use your first name; a lot of spam emails use a single name so recipients can sometimes delete emails like this without realizing they are from 'real' people.

Proper words in proper places make the true definition of a style.

Jonathan Swift

WORK AND FORMAL EMAILS

What is the difference between an email and a letter? Only the technology. Whether they realize they do it or not, people will judge you on your email writing skills. So it is worth taking care when writing emails. A sloppy, confused email suggests that the writer is sloppy, badly organized and couldn't be bothered to make an effort.

Most businesses have policies that cover email use. There may be approved abbreviations, ways of addressing people and so on. Make sure you stick to those rules. Because of the informal nature of emails, things can get written electronically that would never be found in a formal business letter; that can have legal implications, so be careful what you write and to whom.

Many people use a 'signature' for work or business emails. This includes the writer's name, address and contact details. Keep it as short as possible and try to avoid adding logos or links to websites (unless it is your company or personal website). Even if you are writing to people who know you well, it is helpful to leave your contact details on the email so they don't have to look them up if they need them.

Signatures can also contain a short marketing message. Don't make the marketing message so large that it could almost be an email message on its own and make sure it is appropriate to add to your emails; you may need different signatures for work, family, friends and hobbies. Refrain from adding a line of asterisks or hyphens as decoration; if someone with a visual impairment is using text-to-speech software, the computer will read out 'Asterisk, asterisk, asterisk…' which can be infuriating.

- Correct punctuation and spelling is important, as is use of capitals; typing words using ALL CAPITALS IS THE EQUIVALENT OF SHOUTING so don't do it.
- Try to avoid the kind of abbreviations you would see in text messaging (such as BTW and LOL); they are not appropriate in business emails.
- Do not use emoticons in formal emails.
- Keep emails as short as possible; one screen length is ideal.
- If you are responding to an email, copy or highlight the points of the received message that you are responding to.

Insight

Check that you have written a concise, clear email. See if it is possible to scan the email and pick up the main points in five seconds. If it takes longer, redraft the email.

PUNCTUATION IN EMAILS

Full stop

This is used in exactly the same way as any other form of written communication. Also known as a 'dot' when used in email and web addresses (use lower case letters and no space after the dot in these cases).

Ellipsis

These seem to appear frequently in emails. As in conventional writing, the ellipsis can show hesitation, an unfinished sentence or thought, missing words and it adds to the breathy conversational tone. But it also shows that writer hasn't thought through what they want to say. It is as if the ellipsis represents their thinking pauses... they know they haven't finished yet...but are not sure quite where the sentence is going...so they buy themselves some time by slipping in an ellipsis. It's better to plan what you want to say and keep the ellipses to the minimum. Don't use the ellipsis in place of other punctuation.

Hyphens and dashes

If you are unsure whether you should hyphenate a word and you can't find out from a dictionary, remember that hyphenated words (such as 'cry-baby') are easier for the reader to scan than open ones ('cry baby') because they can immediately see which words go together and the meaning you are trying to convey. Dashes often replace full stops, semicolons and colons in emails.

Exclamation marks

These were discussed more fully in Chapter 2 but they are worth mentioning here because they seem to infect blogs, emails and social networking sites like rashes!!! Overuse leads to overkill; more is not better. A single, well-placed exclamation mark is more effective than a load of them. They can also be visually distracting which is annoying for readers. Restrain yourself.

Quotation marks

Where print would normally use italics to distinguish a word or title, the internet sometimes opts for quotation marks. This is because italic text does not always appear correctly online and can be harder to read on a screen, especially if it is just one word that is being italicized.

Whether you use single or double quote marks is up to you, but the single version takes up less space – which can be a consideration, especially in titles.

Abbreviations

Full stops/periods are being used less and less with abbreviations. This is probably due to a direct influence from writing on the internet. Abbreviations without full stops are shorter than ones that have them.

Emoticons

Also known as 'smileys', they are constructed from punctuation marks and are used to help convey a tone of voice. :-) = smiling face :-(= sad face :-p = tongue sticking out ;-) = winking :^0 = surprise. In some word processing programmes, if you type the punctuation marks that traditionally make up an emoticon (for example, a colon, hyphen and bracket) this is automatically translated into a smiley face (☺).

Emoticons are *not* punctuation marks (even if they are composed of them); they go hand in hand with a joke so you should only use them when it is appropriate to make jokes. Emoticons should not appear in formal serious emails; they are fine between friends.

Asides

Another feature of emails are 'asides'. These are types of editorial comments that the writer uses to show their tone of voice or attitude;

for example, <yawn>, <ironic laughter> <LOL>. Like emoticons, they are fine in emails between friends but not for formal, business emails.

Insight

You should never rely on a spellchecker exclusively to pick up errors but they do have their uses. Some email programmes do not have a spellchecking facility. So if you don't have one, copy and paste your email copy into a Word document and check it that way.

Scanning

Online reading is very different from reading the printed word. Internet users do not read text online in the traditional sense (left to right and top to bottom, as they would if reading a book). We jump around the page, scanning the text and pictures quickly, looking for keywords, reading the odd line or phrase, to find things that interested us. We don't turn pages; we scroll through them.

Eye-tracking studies show that people do not read web pages word for word. They scan:

▶ to check whether the content is relevant
▶ the headings, titles, anything in bold
▶ the images.

Web pages are not just made up of words and pictures. There are hyperlinks, moving pictures, sound that can interrupt our concentration and train of thought. Studies show that people skim through the text quickly, sometimes only taking three seconds before they move on to another page or web site. It is extremely unlikely that they will read the majority of the text. You should bear this in mind when writing for web pages.

Research has shown that people view most web pages for 10 seconds or less.

Fewer than 1 in 10 pages viewed are looked at for more than 2 minutes

The Shallows, Nicholas Carr Atlantic Books, 2010

Early websites were heavily influenced by the printed page. Now, printed materials (like magazines and newspapers) have changed their style and layout to mimic that of web pages. Articles are shorter, there are boxed off sections of commentary or bullet pointed facts – making the pages easier to scan.

Scanning takes less effort than reading word for word. Short sentences that have a clear, unambiguous meaning are most likely to grab the reader's attention and hold it, than long, involved sentences.

Websites

Websites are much more than just pages of copy. The design, menus, layout and links all play an important part in how successful a website is. But, even with most people skimming through the text, a well-written website will keep visitors engaged and on your site which is what you want to achieve.

The internet is a wonderful resource for all kinds of information, some of it more reliable than others. Errors, whether they are poor punctuation, bad spelling or faulty grammar, undermines the credibility of a website. And unfortunately there is a lot of poorly written copy on the internet. Unlike newspapers, books and magazines, many websites are not written by professional writers and have no editorial input at all. It is your responsibility to proofread everything you write for the web.

KNOWING WHO YOUR AUDIENCE IS

Ask yourself, why are people going to visit my site? Are they:

▶ searching for information
▶ looking to buy products or services
▶ wanting to learn something
▶ wanting to be amused
▶ asking for advice
▶ communicating with others.

The advantage of a website is that you can get an idea about your visitors by using analytical tools (such as Google Analytics, AWStats, Snoop, etc.). The statistics can show:

▶ where visitors come from
▶ how long they spend on the site
▶ which pages get most traffic
▶ which links are clicked on the most

- ▶ which pages are appearing high in search engines
- ▶ the most popular pages.

From this information, you can make decisions about your marketing objectives, learn what is working and what is not and which pages are highly optimized and therefore show good usability and site navigation.

Perhaps more than any other medium, websites can potentially have truly global audiences. Your target audience may be the retired over 60s in the south of England but do not assume that they will be your only visitors. The age, sex, culture, nationality and preferences of your readers can be far-ranging. It's a fine balancing act of writing for your target audience but not excluding everyone else. (See 'Language' further on.)

Insight

You can apply for an Internet Crystal Mark from the Plain English Society (www.plainenglish.co.uk/internet-crystal-mark.html) to show that you are willing to do everything to make your site clear and easy to read. The Society also has a 'drivel defence' so you can check whether your web pages are written in plain English (www.plainenglish.co.uk/drivel-defence.html).

Did you know?

The World Wide Web Consortium (W3C) issues standards and accessibility guidelines for websites (www.w3.org).

SEO AND KEYWORDS

SEO stands for 'search engine optimization'. These are ways by which websites optimize their pages so that when people are searching for information on the internet, the website appears on the list of possible options. The search engines rank websites and list them from what they see as the most informative and useful to the most obscure. The aim is to get your website ranking as high as possible.

Think of how you search for information on the internet; you will type in one or two words, maybe a short phrase, hit 'enter' and your search engines (Google, Bing, Ask, Yahoo or one of the many other options) will give you pages (sometimes of several thousand websites) of options. Very few people search beyond the first page of results. So the aim is to appear as high up the list as possible and feature on the first page of results.

Search engines are very secretive about how they search for information. The design of a page is important as is the coding of a website. In all, search engines look at around 200 elements before ranking a web page or website. The content of a website is also crucial; search engines like to work through a decent amount of copy to gauge a page's rank. The search engine is particularly looking for the keywords. Keywords help give a website a ranking. The higher the ranking, the higher up the list a website appears (i.e. on the first page of suggested sites).

To find out what keywords would be useful to you, use a keyword search tool, such as Google AdWords or Trellian's Keyword Discovery. The tool will help you pinpoint useful phrases and words for your website. You need keywords that are high in volume and low in difficulty. A keyword with a high difficulty score means that it is extremely common and found on lots of other sites, therefore there is a lot of competition to try to rank it highly.

For example, a keyword like 'cupcakes' is going to have a high difficulty score; even 'designer cupcakes' will be extremely competitive. Neither will help your page ranking. However, making the phrase more specific ('miniature pink cupcakes') will be lower in difficulty, which is what you want to direct traffic (i.e. visitors) to your site. You can combine high and low difficulty words into useful phrases.

Test all the possible keywords using the keyword search tool. When you have built up a list of keywords, you can go through and edit out the least effective ones (high difficulty), the ones that do not really relate to your website and any single word keywords. You should then be left with keywords that you can incorporate into your copy, headlines, page titles to links. Remember:

▶ Repeat the keywords but don't sound repetitive.
▶ The higher the difficulty score, the more repetitions you need to help your ranking.

To analyse a text and give you an idea of what the key words are, copy and paste the words into a Word document. Use the Keyword macro to find out every word that is used in the text and how often it appears. You can use this to see whether you have used keywords enough times or to pick out the words that have been used most, which would indicate what the main keywords are.

- ▶ Repeat keywords throughout the website.
- ▶ Start paragraphs with a keyword so that readers and search engines can pick up the sense of the page quickly.
- ▶ Use phrases that people might type in when searching for a site as part of the body of your text or in titles.
- ▶ Don't use abbreviated keywords; people tend to type out the full word when searching.
- ▶ Use keywords in headings and titles.
- ▶ Make keywords bold or add them to links to highlight them.

Keywords can be single words, several words or phrases; the most effective keywords are, in fact, short phrases. The trick is to capture the exact terms that people are typing into search engines while at the same time producing informative and readable text that keeps people interested.

Insight

When you have written your first draft of web copy, print it and go through it, highlighting the keywords. You can then see how well spread out – or not – they are throughout the text. You may have to edit a few phrases to get the balance right.

Keyword stuffing is when random keywords are added to the title pages. Search engines are not that stupid and will pick up (and rate more highly) a proper phrase or title over the random words.

All writers should be aware of the importance of search engines and keywords. As more people make discoveries through the internet the necessity of including important words within the copy becomes more relevant.

PAGE TITLES

Give some thought to the title of each page. This is the text that appears on the top of the browser window. It can be quite short, running to around 100 characters. It is often the first thing to load onto a computer screen so it tells the visitor what they can expect from that page. If that visitor does not like what they see, then they'll click off the page before it has even finished loading.

Page titles are also important because:

- ▶ search engines use them as part of their rating system
- ▶ they appear in the list of bookmarks and favourites menus
- ▶ they feature on the browser tab and taskbar.

To write an effective page title:

- ▶ Concentrate on the first 65 characters; search engines will index these first and show them on search result pages. These words need to clearly describe what the page contains.
- ▶ Give each page its own title; don't reuse the same one throughout the website.
- ▶ Use words that people would type into search engines.
- ▶ Make sure your keyword or words are early on in the title; don't just lead with your company name.

VOICE OF A WEBSITE

The voice of a website should be consistent throughout the site and be reflected in the text, graphics, images and design. For example, if the purpose is to give information or guidance on something, then the voice should be informative. If the main aim is to sell, then all the elements of the site, including the words, should help prospective buyers come to a decision or make a transaction

Websites, like emails, are suited to a more relaxed, informal approach but it is not appropriate for every site. Contractions, slang and jokey humour will suit some but not others. Work out what your audience would expect from the website. Make sure you get the right level of formality or informality. The design of the website will help dictate this as will the words used.

ONLINE WRITING

- ▶ Keep sentences short and paragraphs short; they are easier to scan.
- ▶ Keep vocabulary fairly simple; it is easier to take in when scanning the page.
- ▶ Make sure headings and titles are clear and explain what the section is about.
- ▶ Err on the side of writing for a lower reading comprehension rather than a more sophisticated level.
- ▶ Front-load the content – the most important facts and information appears in the top left of the page. Also add the most important points at the beginning of paragraphs and sentences.
- ▶ Highlight the important content, such as headings, bold text.
- ▶ Use bulleted lists to help important points stand out.

▶ Keywords will be among the important words. Remember to use keywords when you are labelling images, etc. on the website.
▶ Tables are a good way of displaying important information and add a different visual element to the page.

Don't:

▶ put important information at the bottom of the page
▶ take time making a point
▶ overuse bold text; it is hard to read
▶ use long words which can be misread and misunderstood; some websites are viewed on other devices, like mobile phones
▶ use waffle; keep to the point.

Insight

If you find it difficult to break down a section of text into short paragraphs because of its complexity or because it cannot be cut down, you could add a summary box at the top of the page, where the main points are highlighted using bullet points.

LANGUAGE

The internet is truly international. Bear this in mind when you are producing your website or writing to people in other countries because not everyone has English as their first language. You need to be clear and literal.

For example, it is usual drop some words in English when the meaning is clear (to the native speaker). In the sentence, 'I bought a hat, skirt and blouse for the interview', we have dropped 'a' from skirt and blouse ('I bought a hat, a skirt and a blouse...'). As a sentence, it flows better without the extra a's in it but some of the precision is lost. We are not suggesting that you plod through every sentence, making sure there are no omissions and repeating words over and over; just be aware that if the meaning is slightly unclear, you may lose some of your non-English speakers.

The advantage of writing for a wide audience makes your text easier to understand, both for your target audience and other visitors.

▶ Vocabulary and sentences – keep short, clear and simple.
▶ Use subject – verb – object word order, which is familiar to most readers.
▶ Be general; do not use location-specific terms (e.g. 'our country') – it can alienate visitors.

- ▶ Try to avoid using jargon; if you have to use a technical word, consider giving it a definition.
- ▶ Slang and cultural references – can be hard for people from other countries to understand (e.g. references to cricket or baseball).
- ▶ Spell out shortened words and obscure acronyms.
- ▶ Avoid using simplified text spellings, like 'thru' for 'through' or 'BTW' ('by the way') which can be confusing and look lazy or sloppy.
- ▶ Use gender-neutral terms wherever possible.
- ▶ Don't rely on 'There is…', 'There are…' and 'It is…' too much; it lengthens a sentence and isn't a very strong opening (e.g. instead of 'There is a FAQ section where you can find information', 'Go to the FAQ section for more information').

FONT

Newspapers popularized the use of serif fonts because the curly added bits on each letter gave a top and bottom line for the eye to follow; useful when faced with large blocks of print. Some of the most commonly used fonts are named after newspapers (such as Times).

What works on paper does not always translate to the screen. Web pages are viewed on a computer screen or handheld device. The typeface on a screen is not as high a resolution as a newspaper; although as HD and higher resolution monitors become more common that will start to change. Resolution is measured in 'dpi' (dots per inch). A resolution on most screens is currently around 72 dpi; a newspaper can print text at over 600dpi. So the detail found in serif fonts can be slightly lost when viewed on screen. Using a sans serif font, like Ariel, Monaco or Calibri, is easier for readers of websites.

PUNCTUATION ON WEBSITES

Use punctuation to help make sense of the words but keep it simple. An uncluttered page of text is easier to read than one that is full of punctuation marks. Bloggers are often very sparing with their punctuation which is not always a problem, especially if they are writing informally. 'Hi Joe', 'Way to go Mary', 'Nice one Jim' are fine but, technically, they could all do with a comma in the right place (before each name in this case). If you don't use punctuation you run the risk of ambiguity (exactly what does the writer mean here?) or worse, an unfortunate double meaning ('What's up Lynn' suggests at least two different scenarios).

We looked at punctuation in greater detail in Chapter 2 but it is worth running through the more important punctuation marks, especially when writing blogs, on social networking sites or copy for websites.

- ▶ Comma – a brief pause which helps the reader take in the meaning of the sentence more easily; helps separate words in a list; after or before linking words ('However, we think...'; 'Hi, George', etc.).
- ▶ Full stop – use at the end of every sentence so the reader knows they have come to the end.
- ▶ Capital letters – start a sentence; start the names of people, places, companies, etc.; use for job titles, nationalities, languages, days, months. DO NOT USE IN WHOLE SENTENCES.
- ▶ File names are written in lower case (e.g. exe, jpg) and file types are uppercase (e.g. DOC, GIF).
- ▶ Apostrophe – to show contraction (can't, won't) or possession (it's, the office's memo).
- ▶ Colon – use to introduce items in a list.
- ▶ Exclamation mark – use sparingly, even on an informal site.
- ▶ The slash / (solidus or virgule) is a punctuation mark that indicates a choice between words (and/or). It is also used in URLs. It is becoming better known as a 'forward slash' as opposed to a 'back slash' (\).

NAVIGATION

When you land on a website, you want to be able to move around the pages easily. If you have a website or are planning to put one together, think about what your visitor wants when they click on your site. Don't make things difficult for them. As a guideline, aim for getting to any page on your site in no more than three clicks.

Aim for short pages that have bite-sized paragraphs, using lists and clear headlines; these are the kind of pages that people find are easy to move around.

Divide the content into logical groups. For example:

- ▶ news (latest news, press releases, updates)
- ▶ items for sale

- branch information (location, opening hours, contact numbers)
- reports (financial, legal, etc.)
- contact information for you or your organization.

Contents
Books, newspapers and magazines all have a list of contents. Give your visitors a sense of what the website contains with a contents list.

Contact details
Give an address and phone number as well as an email address. Remember that not everyone has a ZIP code or a postcode. Don't make pull-down address menus country-specific (i.e. the states of USA or English counties)

Text
Now is not the time to indulge in weird and wonderful fonts; stick to something familiar and clear.

- Text appears differently on screen than it does on paper. Check out how the typeface looks on both the screen and hard copy.
- Screen sizes vary from user to user and it is not always easy to control what size your text will appear on all screens. However, try not to use more than 70 characters in a line of text; people can then read without having to scroll from left to right.

Links & labelling
Write clear text links so people know where they are, what you want them to do (for example, 'Print' and 'Next Page') and what will happen. Describing what the link is ('Contact me', 'Directions', 'Terms & conditions') rather than 'Click here' is useful for all your website visitors. It is also important because the visually impaired often use a screen reader, which converts text to speech; in other words, the visitor will hear the words used for the link. 'Click here' does not tell them where the link will take them.

- Use the same words in your link text as the page heading where the link takes you, e.g. the link is 'Home' which takes you to the page, headed 'Home'.
- Use keywords in the link text where you can.
- Use helpful descriptive words, rather than 'More' or 'Next' which don't tell you anything.
- Be consistent; use the same commands throughout the website ('Select' or 'Enter') for ease of navigation.

Text links should come under the same rules of punctuation and grammar. If the link falls in the middle of a sentence, <u>such as this one</u>, use lower case letters. The exceptions to using correct punctuation are:

▶ You can use upper case and write links as headings (many sites do because they are so familiar to users); just be consistent. Examples are: Terms & Conditions, About Us, Contact Us.
▶ If the link is part of a sentence (<u>like this</u>) and comes at the end of it, you can add a full stop (or ?/!). If the link is written as a URL (e.g. <u>www.hodder.co.uk</u>) don't put a full stop at the end in case people think it is part of the URL. Adding a stray full stop to a URL can result in a broken link.
▶ If the link is not part of a sentence and stands alone, you do not have to use end punctuation.

Some, but not all, internet browsers incorporate a spellchecker that can scan any text you enter onto a website.

Alt text

Alt text is a description of an image on a website. Label things clearly on your site, including images; describe what it is ('Head Office', 'chicken coop', 'athletics stadium', for example, rather than 'jpg 23423'). Alt text appears first, before the image has fully loaded. This is ideal for the visually impaired; the alt text will be read out loud by the computer's screen reader. Search engines also pick up alt text words, which will help with SEO.

▶ Keep the alt text phrases short.
▶ Don't use generic alt text throughout the site; give each image is own alt text description.
▶ Avoid jargon and marketing spiel.
▶ Don't be vague with the descriptions; if you have a picture of an envelope by your address, don't describe it as 'Letter', call it 'Write to us' or 'Our address'.

Consistency

Use the same terms and format throughout the site. It can be confusing if you have 'Contact us' on one page and 'Our address' on another if they are exactly the same.

FAQ (frequently asked questions)

Often one of the best-written parts of a website because the writer has had to consider things from the reader's point of view. The focus is completely on the reader (Chapter 4 has more information on writing questions).

EDITING

When writing copy for websites, write in a word-processing document and edit/proofread from that. It is easier to make changes in this document, rather than a content-publishing tool. Do a final check in the format the words are going to appear in.

Proofreading

In 2002, a study at the Stanford University Persuasive Technology Lab (*How Do People Evaluate a Web Site's Credibility? Results from a Large Study*) found that typos were one of the top ten factors that reduced a website's credibility.

We look at proofreading in more detail in Chapter 9 but it is worth touching on here. When proofreading emails, websites and blogs, you should:

- ▶ check spelling, omissions, grammar
- ▶ check links to see that they are active and work
- ▶ make sure videos, slideshows and photos can be viewed
- ▶ look out for words that may be displayed incorrectly (e.g. HermE instead of Hermé); characters such as accents may need to be coded in order to appear correctly
- ▶ check any bold or italics are being displayed properly (e.g. they may not work in a plain text email).

Blogging

The word 'blog' is made up of two words: 'web' and 'log'. A blog can take the form of a diary (which many of the first blogs were), a source of news or a stream of consciousness. It can be made up of text, photos, audio or video. Whether used for personal or business use, the style is often casual and conversational.

Technorati.com is a search engine for blogs. By 2008, it had indexed nearly 113 million blogs around the world. If you want to get a feel for blogs, especially those in the area of writing that you are interested in, go to the website to get an idea of how other bloggers are writing. The idea is not to copy them but see what works and what doesn't.

Just because a blog has a relaxed, chatty feel is no excuse to ignore the rules of grammar and spelling. Think of your reader; it is easier for them to follow your thoughts if your writing is clear and makes sense. Poorly written text (with misspellings and bad grammar) is actually harder to read.

Insight

Search engines will often rank words found in the titles of blog posts higher than words in the blog itself. Make sure your titles are informative.

Organizations like to incorporate blogs into their marketing because the blogs make them seem friendly and approachable (less corporate, in other words) and it is a user-friendly way to circulate news to customers and clients. Even in a 'business' blog, it is acceptable to use the first person, 'I' and 'my', which is unusual in most corporate writing. The blog represents your company and, no matter how friendly or relaxed you want it to be, it has to have a professional gloss *and* tone as well.

Insight

Even if you write your blog with a specific audience in mind, remember that the internet is a public space and *anyone* can access what you have written. Work out what you want to reveal about yourself, what you are happy for people to know.

WHY WRITE A BLOG

What are your reasons for writing a blog?

▶ Do you want to be part of a community?
▶ Do you want to change something?
▶ Influence other people?
▶ Or just have a bit of fun?

Working out *why* you want to write can help you with the content and tone.

Some people believe they are successful bloggers if they attract a large audience. Others may write to build a presence for their products or services. Some may just want the discipline of writing on a regular basis.

Some bloggers have gone onto get book deals, had films made about them and made money from their blog, (Julia Powell's blog about cooking every recipe in Julia Child's *Mastering the Art of French*

Cooking was turned into a book and then a film; Kyle MacDonald blogged about successfully trading a paperclip for a house which was turned into a book, *One Red Paperclip*) but they are the exception. First and foremost, a blog has to appeal to an audience so that they read what you write. Write, therefore, with your audience in mind.

First of all, decide on the subject you are going to write about. What are you trying to say? Will people be interested in the day-to-day minutiae of your life? Not necessarily unless you happen to be famous. You need to write from a specific point of view: a townie sophisticate who has upped and moved to the country, a lover of good food, someone searching for a job, a traveller's tale... If you write from a specific standpoint, you have a hook, a unique selling point, that people can respond to. That will help make your blog stand out from all the others. Like a newspaper, the content should be different from your competitors, even if you are covering a similar topic.

Writing on a specific subject dictates the kind of words you use in your blog. The vocabulary is important because of keywords. If you want to see whether you are being picked up by search engines, type in some keywords + 'blog' and see if your blog comes up. You can also check out other blogs that deal with similar subjects and see how you compare.

Keywords in blogs are particularly important if you are blogging for a business. You need to make sure that you are including words that people will be using to search for subjects they are interested in.

Insight

Read your blog out loud before you post it online. Most blogs aim for a chatty, conversational style. If you find it easy to read aloud, you have got the tone right and it will be easy for people to read.

WHEN TO WRITE

A good blog is written regularly. If you stick to a timetable of sorts, your readership knows when to expect something new. If you blog infrequently, your audience will lose interest or will be less inclined to engage in a dialogue with you.

► A good blogger updates their posts regularly. That doesn't have to be every day but do post something at least once a month, once a week is better.

▶ The writing bug does not always strike at the best times so stockpile a few blogs that you can use when you are either short of time, on holiday or have no inspiration.

LONG OR SHORT?

Bloggers seem to be divided about whether to keep blogs short or not. Certainly, short seems to be the norm in most internet copy; it keeps your reader's interest and it fits onto the screen in one go. The advantage of a longer blog is that you can develop your argument or theme; you are not constricted by space and length. A longer post also keeps your reader on site for longer.

The subject matter probably dictates whether you can get away with a short or a long post. Again, look at other bloggers and see what they do. Who has got it right? What works for your subject?

Insight

Rather than write directly onto your blog site, first write your post in Word or Notepad. You can rewrite, edit and play around with it here before you are happy with it. Save it and then copy and paste into your blog software. You don't want to spend time and effort crafting a really good entry only to find that there has been some technical problem, your post has been lost and you have to start again from scratch.

When you paste into your blog software, you are usually able to format the copy here. Most software programs allow you to add bold, italics, underline, change the font, the size and so on. You can format lists at this point and concentrate on making the blog look good.

WHEN A BLOG IS POSTED

When you publish a blog, the following happens:

▶ The new post appears at the top of your blog's home page.
▶ The software adds the new blog to the archive.
▶ An email notification is sent out to people who have signed up to your blogs.
▶ Some blog software will notify search engines that a new post has appeared.

So when you publish a post, it goes live immediately. Re-read, edit and check carefully before you are happy with what you have written. Even if you recall it, to amend a typo or change a fact, the original post will still have been published and probably read by someone.

BLOG WEB SERVICES

You do not need to set up your own website to run a blog; there are several services that allow you to blog through them; Wordpress.com is one, Blogger.com is another. Some hosts are free; others do charge. Shop around to find one that provides you with the services that you want. Using a hosted blog service:

▶ your blog will be hosted on their server which is reliable and gives off-site back up

▶ you can get web (and mobile) access from anywhere

▶ provides templates so the blog looks professional

▶ provides many offer widgets (small panels of information to the side of the page that draw information from other sources, such as Facebook, Twitter or Flickr – useful to link your social media accounts/website to your blog)

▶ is easy for novice bloggers to start using.

NAMING YOUR BLOG

Look at other examples of what people have called their blog. Which ones do you think work well? Why are some unsuccessful? Generally, the ones that work are those that clearly describe the tone and content of a blog.

ABOUT ME SECTION

Most blogs have an 'About me' section where readers can find out a bit about you and what your blog is all about. This is just a brief introduction. If you have got anything more to say, put it in your blog.

SHARING

A blog is not just a one-sided affair. The best blogs are like conversations with input from the blogger and the readership. By encouraging people to comment on your blog, you build your audience.

- ▶ Readers can spark new ideas for your blog.
- ▶ Reply to someone if they ask questions or make comments.
- ▶ Always thank them for getting in touch.
- ▶ Comment on other people's blogs; it encourages them and their readers to look at your blog.
- ▶ Ask open-ended questions to encourage people to comment.

THINGS TO DO WHEN BLOGGING

The layout of your blog is important; make it easy for people to scan quickly when they read it. They are more likely to read what you have written.

- ▶ Use header tags to separate the sections in your blog; lists also help break up the text and make it easy to scan and take in the information.
- ▶ Read and contribute to other people's blogs.
- ▶ Use keywords in the titles the main text.
- ▶ Aim for a conversational tone.
- ▶ Check your grammar and spelling, even when being chatty, you want to be understood.

THINGS TO AVOID WHEN BLOGGING

- ▶ Don't use long sentences or long paragraphs; they make it harder to scan the text.
- ▶ Do not share any personal identification online, including anything that you might use as a password (pet's name, mother's maiden name, etc.).

Useful websites

- ▶ www.problogger.net – articles on how to improve your blog, includes tips on making money, writing content and other tips.
- ▶ www.copyblogger.com – gives information on developing content for blogs.

Twitter and tweets

It's been said that Facebook is for people you already know and Twitter is for people you want to know.

Don Sagolla, *140 Characters* (Wiley 2009).

<u>Twitter.com</u> is a free social networking site used for microblogging. It is not the only microblogging platform but it is perhaps the best known (with currently over 145 million registered users). Faster – and shorter – than conventional blogging, texting what amounts to a couple of sentences and no more, Twitter has grown in popularity due to its ease, entertainment value and immediacy.

It is a mixture of instant messaging and blogging. So you can let people know what you are up to and follow others – whether you know them or not – to see what they are doing. Type in an entry (or 'tweet') and it appears instantly, either on a computer or mobile phone.

While a tweet is effectively an answer to the question 'What is happening?' people use Twitter in a variety of ways.

- ▶ **Businesses** – let customers know about special offers, a new product launch, to network.
- ▶ **Organizations** – keep members informed of news, network, promote events.
- ▶ **Celebrities** – like a product, they are promoting themselves.
- ▶ **Politicians** – another form of canvassing; keeping voters informed.
- ▶ **Friends** – keeping in touch.
- ▶ **Ordinary people** – reporting on extraordinary events.

'For sale: baby shoes, never worn' is a six-word story that is attributed to Ernest Hemingway. Whether he was responsible for it or not, it illustrates how so few words can conjure up a much bigger and more powerful idea.

Each post (or message) is limited to 140 characters (letters, numbers, spaces and symbols). It is that very constraint that can be challenging. How to be witty, informative, thought-provoking – or whatever you are aiming at – in so few words is an art. Advertising copywriters and headline writers have perfected that art; successful twitterers are just as succinct and creative.

To help create space for your message:

▶ Minimize adverbs and articles.
▶ Commas are not always necessary.
▶ You can do without personal pronouns.
▶ Use contractions and symbols (like &, £, @).
▶ Shortened forms of letters (like 'thru', 'lite') are acceptable.
▶ Avoid over-using exclamation marks.
▶ All capital letters are the equivalent of shouting.
▶ All lower case letters don't save characters; that is just being lazy.
▶ Don't use negativity; if you've written 'can't' or 'don't', try to turn the sentence into a positive rather than a negative. It usually takes fewer characters as well.
▶ Alliteration works well in tweets (being brief and bold is better than bored).
▶ As does onomatopoeia, such as 'Psst' or 'Grr' (more information on this in Chapter 9).

Did you know?

Phillipa Gregory, author of *The White Queen*, tweeted the book daily over 3 weeks so that people had the experience of reading the story in instalments. Written in the first-person, present-tense, each tweet had to be carefully written. It was, Gregory acknowledges, a 'formidable piece of work to write the tweets.'

VOICE

Is your Twitter account for business or pleasure? What are you happy to share with people? What would you prefer to keep private?

▶ Whether you are writing as yourself or on behalf of a business, remember that tweeting is a conversation. It is not all about you; there is a strong element of give and take, talking and listening.
▶ Sarcasm and irony feature strongly in a lot of social media but this should not be the only tone to take. There is nothing wrong with being open, honest and sincere.
▶ The type of voice you project will be, in part, reflected in the name that you choose to use for your Twitter account.

NAME

You need a descriptive name but one that uses as few characters as possible. Think of it as your stage name. If you use your real name, it can be hard to distinguish yourself from everyone else, especially if you have a fairly common name.

▶ How do you want to be perceived? Does your name reflect that?
▶ Have a friendly, accessible name; don't be weird or rude.
▶ Keep the name short; the longer the name the less room for your message (Twitter limits user names to 15 characters).
▶ If you want to use a Twitter account for a business, think about using strong keywords for your Twitter name; SEO works on Twitter accounts as well because each tweet is effectively a web page in its own right.

AUDIENCES AND WHEN TO TWEET

On Facebook, you are broadcasting to people who you want to be your friend; with Twitter, you are broadcasting to everyone. Know who your audience is. Or at least, work out who you want to have as an audience and address your tweets to them. Limit the vocabulary of your tweets to your audience; it helps to build focus and a following.

▶ Whoever your audience is, avoid drunken, late night tweets; don't tweet when you are angry.
▶ Be genuine and pleasant to followers; don't be a troll.
▶ There is such a thing as tweeting too much. You do not have to tweet every hour of the day.

Look at other tweets in the subject area that you are interested in. Search for them using keywords. When you have found people you would like to tweet to, engage them in conversation. You cannot build an audience or followers if you just observe from the sidelines. A person with a lot of followers is called a leader. Lady Gaga, the singer, was the first user to get over 10 million followers.

You cannot control who follows you. You may have started out as a passionate baker of bread who wants to share their love of dough with other cooks; but you could attract a completely different kind of follower. That is not a bad thing whether you are a business or an individual; businesses can attract a new customer base, while individuals are engaging with different people and expanding their horizons.

188

WHAT TO TWEET

Ideally, all tweets should be fascinating but even the most brilliant writer will struggle for excellence every time. Try to avoid telling people what you had for breakfast or the dreadful journey to work. Listening can help you decide what to tweet about. People want to read about:

▶ what you think about the latest news
▶ your interests.

Avoid mentioning:

▶ personal details (children's names, address, telephone numbers)
▶ financial details
▶ anything that is confidential
▶ politics, sex and religion (if you are tweeting as a business).

Insight

Don't give too much away. England cricketer Kevin Pietersen was fined for comments on Twitter after he was dropped from the one-day team; while Olympic gold-medallist swimmer, Stephanie Rice of Australia, lost a lucrative sponsorship deal following comments she made on Twitter.

If you are tweeting for a business, remember that tweets are conversations; you are interacting with your customers and staff, not just firing marketing messages at them. It is a very different type of corporate communication, one that, to an extent, businesses have no control over; anyone can comment back. So make sure you do listen as well as promote. Never send out spam. A good ratio is to do promotional tweets about ten per cent of the time; the rest should be general comments, entertaining news and ideas.

However difficult or enjoyable, it is still important that the message is clear and can be understood. Keep to one message per tweet; don't be tempted to try to extend a thought, idea or subject over several tweets because:

▶ the messages could arrive appear out of order
▶ it is difficult to refer to or link a list of messages together; you just don't have enough space.

PROOFREAD

Yes, even for 140 characters. It's because it is so short that communicating clearly and concisely is important and for that you need to follow the rules of grammar. You have to make an impression in a short time. You will be judged on one tweet or text.

RETWEET

A retweet is when someone forwards or comments on your tweet. It is considered good manners if you credit the original tweeter.

The more characters you use, the less space there is for others to forward and comment on your post. So, if you can limit your tweet to 120 characters, you are helping others to repost it, with your username. If you can get the post down to 100 characters, you are leaving even more space for your followers.

▶ Type 'Please retweet'; the message will be picked up and re-transmitted by retweet bots.
▶ 'Please retweet' can be used by the next writer and passed on to others.
▶ Don't demand to be retweeted; always be polite and ask nicely.
▶ Retweet and republish other people's tweets; they may do the same to you.

Text messaging

An SMS (Short Message Service) text can be sent from mobile phones. Text messages were traditionally limited to 160 characters or less; anything longer brought additional costs. Text allowances are more generous now and for many mobile users there is no extra cost if they go over 160 characters. Nevertheless, old habits die hard and we continue to send short, brief texts ('Thx 4 yr msg. Will CUL8R'; see more examples later).

Insight

If you wanted to emphasize a word, enclose it between *asterisks* rather than use italics or bold which do not always show up on the screen. You can also use the lesser and greater symbols when you want to add an aside <if you know what I mean>.

When you write a text message, remember that you are writing for a very small screen. Although smart phones have larger screens, a lot of people still have traditional mobile phones with screens that only show a few lines of text. Your reader does not want to have to scroll through lines and lines of text so short texts are better.

- Because texts (and tweets) had so few characters to play with, users learned to take out vowels to shorten the words (text = txt). Some punctuation marks, like apostrophes, are also easy to jettison to save space; this is acceptable practice.
- If a word or part of a word can be represented by a number (for = 4, forgive = 4give, later = L8R), this also saves characters.
- Symbols are also useful to keep messages short (& = and, @ = at, % = per cent)
- Days of the week and months of the year can be abbreviated (Mon, Tue, Wed, Jan, Feb, Mar).
- Time can be represented as 2hr 30m; don't use a colon to separate the numbers (2:30) because it could be mistaken for the time of day, rather than a length of time.
- If a word can be represented by a one or two characters (why = Y, any = NE).
- Combining the abbreviations allows you to write words with few characters (Anyone = NE1).

Did you know?

Over 2 trillion text messages are sent worldwide every year. (*The Shallows: How the Internet Is Changing the Way We Think, Read and Remember*, Nicholas Carr, Atlantic, 2010)

Common text phrases

BRB	Be right back
BTW	By the way
CUL8R	See you later
LOL	Laugh/s(ing) out loud
MSG	Message
PLZ	Please
TY	Thank you
THX	Thanks
b/c	because
BFN	bye for now
BTW	by the way
DM	direct message
EM	email
FB	Facebook
FTF/F2F	face to face

LI	LinkedIn
LMK	let me know
NP	no problem
PLZ	please
RT	retweet
TMB	tweet me back

<3 = text version of a heart

Did you know?

LOL (laughing out loud) was added to the *Oxford English Dictionary* in 2011 with the definition 'used chiefly in electronic communications to draw attention to a joke or humorous statement, or to express amusement'. The French version of 'LOL' is 'mdr' (mort de rire = 'dying of laughter'); while the Thais use '555' ('5' in Thai is pronounced 'ha'; hence three fives = ha ha ha)

'LOL' and 'OMG' (Oh my God/Oh my goodness) are often the first text abbreviations that people pick up; the text equivalent of a baby's first words. They are quickly typed on a qwerty keyboard, are simple and multipurpose (can be used humorously, sarcastically, to soften a phrase). Just as laughter in conversation helps the tone, adding 'LOL' lets the reader know when someone is being humorous.

Abbreviations

For some, text abbreviations are a sort of secret code, a badge of belonging. For others, who have mobiles with QWERTY keyboards and an unlimited text allowance, abbreviations are a bit passé.

Abbreviations are, however, ideal for keeping messages short so people do not have to scroll through a long text. But remember who you are texting, only use abbreviations if you are sure that your recipient knows what they mean.

Smileys/emoticons

Smileys, e.g. ☺, are fairly straightforward but they are rather childish. They are being replaced with actual smiley face graphics.

Punctuation

Text messaging is not heavy with punctuation; what there is is used informally. Dashes often replace full stops and commas which are harder to see on small screens. Exclamation marks are also popular – one is fine, any more looks desperate.

BUSINESS TEXTS

Many organizations use texts for marketing messages. Keep the message short and to the point and do not lapse into teenage text speak. You would not have 'txt spk on ur' company website so it is not appropriate here either.

▶ Keep them simple, clear and concise.
▶ Don't try to cram too many ideas and facts into each message.
▶ Make sure your recipient knows who the text message is from.

Insight
If you do not understand what the sender of a text message is trying to say to you (too many abbreviations, perhaps?), just reply with '?'. They will soon get the message.

Double meanings
The space limitation of texting and tweeting can lead to double meanings. Nouns can be mistaken for verbs and vice versa; small, seemingly unimportant words are left out – and this can cause confusion and unintentional amusement. One example (probably apocryphal but makes the point nevertheless) from the days of the telegram (an old-fashioned form of communication where space was at a premium) illustrates this. An editor reputedly sent a telegram to the Hollywood actor, Cary Grant, asking 'How old Cary Grant?' to which Grant replied, 'Old Cary Grant fine. How you?' Dropping the verb ('is') from the first telegram may have saved the editor a bit of money but it altered the sense of the sentence.

Social networking

Social networking websites are places where people get together to share information, opinions and to keep in touch with friends, family, fans and customers. Some of the better known sites are currently:

- Facebook
- Bebo
- MySpace
- LinkedIn
- Friendster
- Orkut
- Twitter
- Plaxo
- QQ
- Gather

People can get in touch with you, either by emailing you directly or posting entries on your page that can be seen by everyone else; it is a bit like leaving a message on a noticeboard at work or college.

Many of the social networking sites have a section where you can blog or write something more substantial than a few sentences. As with any copy, you should review it, check for typos and any anomalies or confusion before posting it. On Facebook, for example, if you are writing in Notes, click 'Preview' (or 'Save Draft' if you have not finished) so you can check over your text and make any changes. When you are happy with what you have written, click 'Publish'.

For more information, go to the social media guide, Mashable. The website (www.mashable.com) provides up-to-the-minute information, trends and news about social media sites.

YOUR PROFILE

Whatever social networking site you use, you need a profile of yourself. This is a way of introducing yourself to people, giving them an idea of what is important to you and represents the kind of person you are.

If you are creating a profile of yourself as a private individual then just be yourself. If you are creating a profile for a product, service or your business, work out what you want to achieve by having a profile. Is it feedback from customers or spreading information?

- Encourage feedback.
- Keep your profile updated; people like to see new information.
- Give proper information about yourself or the company/brand/product.
- Don't use slogans or corporate-speak.
- Don't mislead; be honest.

CHATTING ON SOCIAL NETWORKING SITES

Instant messaging (IM) is computer chat that allows you to have a typed conversation, in real time, with others on the internet. Facebook, Bebo, MySpace and other social networking sites use IM services.

Instant messaging is generally informal, using abbreviations and idiom that would not suit a more formal writing situation. That is not a problem as one as long realizes that there are times when an informal approach is fine (chatting with friends) and others when one should be more correct and use appropriate language ('chatting' on behalf of your company).

In 'real' life, you can have a conversation with a friend – either face to face or on the phone – that remains private. In many social networking sites, you can have an instantaneous chat with a friend that can be read by everyone. Remember that when you are commenting on someone else's site/wall.

Internet forums

Forums and chat rooms are slightly different from one another. A chat room is a 'live' event; people posting comments and have a live conversation with one another. With a forum, you can post comments and/or respond to them over a period of time; the conversation does not take place in real time.

Thriving in cyberspace

The internet has a relaxed feel, an immediacy about it. But that should not encourage carelessness or substandard language. In the internet world, everybody is a writer and a publisher. We should make the effort to be an editor as well. That means checking over what we are writing, looking at it for its content, accuracy, clarity. We have to judge whether it is entertaining, appropriate, will provoke the response we want or avoid offending people.

10 THINGS TO TRY

1 Describe various situations you find yourself in but only use ten words or less.

2 Write a précis of the top news stories – using 120 characters.

3 Build up your texting vocabulary; there are numerous 'dictionaries' on the internet.

4 Study the subject lines of emails you receive; do they accurately describe the contents of the email? Which ones are successful? Which ones don't work?

5 Start to analyse some of your favourite websites. Why do you like them? Study the copy; is it short, easy to read? Should there be more or less? Work out why the site is successful.

6 Go through your company/your own/a favourite website, analyse the keywords.

7 Set up your own blog and start blogging. Aim to post at least once a week.

8 Look at other blogs online; start interacting with the ones that appeal to you.

9 Try to have an email conversation with a friend but only use the subject line.

10 Set up an account on a microblogging site or social network site.

9

Improve your writing

In this chapter you will learn:
- *how to proofread and edit*
- *how to improve your spelling and build your vocabulary*
- *about writing myths*
- *about being a better writer.*

> *People think I can teach them style. What stuff it is. Have something to say and say it as clearly as you can. That is the only secret of style.*

Matthew Arnold

In 1906, the Fowler brothers published *The King's English*, an influential book on English usage and grammar. In the opening chapter, on the first page, they wrote:

> *Any one who wishes to become a good writer should endeavour, before he allows himself to be tempted by the more showy qualities, to be direct, simple, brief, vigorous, and lucid.*

That is still good advice. Writing is about communication. To make sure that one is communicating effectively, the meaning of what has been written must be clear. Ambiguity can confuse or leave the reader with completely the wrong impression. As well as a good grasp of grammar and punctuation, a writer should be able to choose the right words (precise and accurate) and put over their argument concisely and lucidly. All that comes with practice. Writing is a craft which means it can be learned and improved upon. This chapter looks at making yourself a better writer.

Read

Good writers are good readers. Read different styles and different mediums. Read publications and books that are unfamiliar to you; widen your reading horizons. As you read, you can see how an experienced writer deals with punctuation, how they keep the story or meaning of the piece moving forward.

Rewrite

It is extremely unlikely that any writer can produce the perfect draft in one sitting. Professional, experienced writers will write, rewrite and possibly rewrite several times again. It is the only way to achieve a quality product. Whatever you write and however short it is, you should be prepared to go back and rewrite some (if not all) of it.

There is no such thing as a bad first draft – it is a *first* draft. A work in progress. At least you have actually put some words down in some shape and form. Now you can begin to work to improve it.

Insight

Accept that rewriting is part of the writing experience. Think of it as a creative opportunity to improve your writing, rather than a chore that has to be endured. When you read your work back to yourself, pretend it is someone else's. Look at it critically through an editor's eye.

Proofreading and editing

Proofreading and editing are part of the same process but are two slightly different things. Proofreading is about locating any errors such as misspellings and typos. Editing is amending text, changing content and making sure that the writer has said what they want to say in the most effective and clear way. Good editing cannot be seen. The words flow perfectly. Every writer, no matter how good or bad they are, professional or unprofessional, needs editing. Some writers have the luxury of an editor looking at their work; others have to be both writer and editor.

Editing can often help a piece of writing by removing words, sentences or even whole paragraphs. A writer can get very precious about what they have written. They are understandably reluctant to see any of their hard work removed. But they also have to acknowledge that a judicious cut can do wonders for a piece of writing.

▶ Don't try to write and edit; do one at a time.
▶ Take out anything that does not support your argument or focus.
▶ Remove the weakest lines, quotations and anecdotes; this makes what is left even stronger.
▶ Look out for and cut phrases that state the obvious (for example, 'in this report'); adverbs that intensify rather than modify (for example, 'extremely', 'just', 'completely'); jargon and clichés.
▶ Take out any sentences you have to read twice and reword them; if you have to look at them twice, so will your reader.
▶ Have you done what you said you would do; i.e. have you attached documents or given address details?

As well as checking for typing errors, you should be looking at the flow and sense of the text. What does the reader need to know? Have you addressed that? Have you managed to achieve what you set out to do? Ask yourself:

▶ Is it interesting?
▶ Is the message clear?
▶ Is it true? Are the facts correct?
▶ Is there anything I can take out? Be ruthless.
▶ How does it look? Are headings, font, point size consistent. Layout, quality of print out, paper, etc.

Whether you are writing a great novel in your garden shed or sweating over the annual report to the board at work, writing is a solitary existence. It can therefore be helpful to get the opinions of others. This is an important part of the editing process. You need people whose judgement you trust and who appreciate words and the work you are doing. If you do ask for advice or an opinion, be very clear what you want from this person. Ask them:

▶ Where do you think it is good?
▶ Where do you think it is bad?
▶ Where do you think it is slow/confusing?

If you are asking for feedback, make sure that they actually do get back to you with their comments within a reasonable time. You may have a deadline to meet and you do not want to be wasting valuable editing/rewriting time waiting for their response.

When you do get their comments, what you choose to do with them is up to you. You can amend what you have written, or you can disagree with them and ignore what they suggest.

> **Insight**
>
> If you are writing a book, you can go to a literary consultant who will assess and give feedback on a writer's manuscript for a fee. Choose carefully. Literary consultancies should be there to help you make money (by selling your book) rather than just take your money. There is a range of literary consultants in the UK (they are less common in the US); Cornerstones, Hilary Johnson, The Literary Consultancy and The Writer's Journey are some of the better known ones (further details are in the Appendix).

Proofreading is the last stage of your writing. It is the opportunity to make your words free from any errors or confusion. You are looking for misspellings, typing errors, misused words, incorrect facts and, depending on what or to whom you are writing, legal issues. An error-free article keeps your reader focused on the words and not on the mistakes. Even a small mistake can be distracting.

Ideally, you should leave your writing for as long as possible before going back and proofreading. Sometimes, the pressures of work do not allow you do walk away for days or weeks but try to leave as long a gap as possible. Even making a drink or having a short break can help. You come back to your words with fresh eyes.

▶ You need to be able to concentrate when proofreading. Make sure there are no distractions or background noise to disturb you.
▶ Allow enough time to do this properly.
▶ Print out what you have written on your computer; words look different on the printed page than they do on screen.
▶ Reading out loud means you have to read every word; this can pick up any unusual rhythms, odd punctuation and missing words.
▶ Let the computer read your work back to you. Use a software package designed for visually impaired users that reads text. This will not pick up all spelling errors but you can catch missing or peculiar words.
▶ You may have to proofread several times; once to check spelling and grammar, another to check the formatting is consistent, another for the flow and sense of the words.
▶ Take a line of text at a time. It can be helpful to use a ruler or a piece of paper under each line to help concentrate.

- ▶ Read backwards, from the bottom of the page to the top, line by line. When you read forwards, the brain knows what should be coming and can jump over errors without noticing them
- ▶ If you have written instructions, check that they are clear and correct (have any steps been missed out? Are any ingredients or elements missing?).
- ▶ Get someone else to proofread your work.

Spelling

My spelling is Wobbly. It's good spelling but it Wobbles, and the letters get in the wrong places.

AA Milne, *Winnie the Pooh*

In languages such as German, what you see is how you pronounce the word. In English, what you see is not necessarily how it is pronounced. More than a tenth of English words are not spelt the way they sound (such as 'subtle' or 'drought'). Words that are spelt the same can sound quite different (for example, 'dough' – 'tough') which can be difficult for people who have only heard them spoken and not seen written down. And some words are homonyms; they sound the same but are spelled differently ('aloud/allowed'; 'plane/plain' – see later for more examples).

Being able to spell well is an accomplishment that reflects positively on the writer. If a reader comes across spelling mistakes, they will either think the writer is careless, ignorant, lazy – or all three.

One of the most famous spelling 'rules' is that you put an 'i' before an 'e' except after 'c'. It is typical of the English language that, as with any rule, there are exceptions. It does not apply to words like 'foreign', 'science', 'species' and 'ancient'. Where you *can* apply the rule is with words where the 'ie' or 'ei' make an 'ee' sound, such as 'receive', 'achieve' and 'deceive'.

In the Appendix, there is a list of words that are commonly misspelled. Have a look through to familiarize yourself with them. You may also find that you have a tendency to misspell certain words all the time. If that is the case, use the Auto Correct feature on your computer to override your incorrect spelling with the correct one.

All computers have spellcheckers which are useful for spelling (and grammar) on a very basic level. If the computer comes across a word it is not sure about, it will put a wiggly coloured line underneath so you have a visual flag that warns you something may not be right. Use them as your first stage of proofreading. Most are pretty basic in that they check words in isolation, rather than in the context of a sentence. For example, typing the following sentence:

▶ The whether was lovely while they were at there villa.

The computer queried the spelling of 'whether' but missed 'there' completely. Another example of computer 'blindness' is the following rhyme:

I have a spell cite programme
Its part of my win doze
It plainly marks for my revue
Ear ors I did knot no
I've run this poem on it
Its letter purr fact you sea
Sew I don't have to worry
My pee see looks after me

Jonathan Gabay, www.jonathangabay.com, from *Improve your Copywriting*,
(Hodder Education, 2011)

In other words, the computer can pick up some misspelled words but not misused homonyms. It would, for example, have difficulty distinguishing between 'loose /lose', 'passed/past' and 'desert/dessert'. Common homonyms are:

▶ Its, it's
▶ There, their, they're
▶ To, too, two
▶ Grate, great
▶ Knew, new
▶ Bare, bear
▶ Forth, fourth
▶ Seem, seam
▶ Hole, whole

If you would like to know more, look at *Improve Your Spelling* (from the Teach Yourself series) which helps you master the art of spelling and boost your confidence when writing.

Words

The difference between the right word and almost the right word is the difference between lightning and the lightning bug [firefly].

Mark Twain

Everyone has pet hates of words. Jonathon Swift hated 'mob' and 'banter'; while Benjamin Franklin disliked seeing the word 'progress' used as a verb. Most of the time, these are just personal dislikes rather than a cast iron rule that you must never use it.

A wide vocabulary helps to avoid using the same words over and over again. You avoid repetition by using synonyms (definition: different words but with similar or identical meanings – see 'Thesaurus' later). If you wanted to avoid using the verb 'ask', you could go to the Thesaurus, which is a directory of synonyms, to find substitutes. For example, synonyms of ask (verb):

> *Enquire, ask, want to know, not know; demand; request; canvass, agitate, air, ventilate, discuss, bring in question, subject to examination; argue, ask for, look for, enquire for, seek, search for, hunt for, pursue, enquire into, probe, delve into, dig into, dig down into, go deep into; investigate, conduct an enquiry, hold an enquiry, institute an enquiry, set up an enquiry, throw open to enquiry, get to the bottom of, fathom, see into, scan, be curious, survey, reconnoitre, explore, feel one's way, sample, taste, examine oneself, take a look at.*

Roget's Thesauraus, 6th edition (Longman, 1972)

That is a huge list to choose from and many of the words will be inappropriate. But others will sit happily in your sentence and may trigger an idea, a metaphor or image that will invigorate your writing.

THESAURUS

'Thesaurus' is Greek for 'treasure house'. First published in 1852 by P.M. Roget, the Thesaurus is a lexicon of English synonyms or near-synonyms (a lexicon is the vocabulary of a language, including words and expressions). A synonym is a word that means the same thing as another (e.g. 'rain' and 'drizzle').

A thesaurus helps a writer find a substitute for a word that is close in meaning. In a thesaurus, the words are not arranged in an A–Z set-up but according to the ideas they express. Each word is organized into categories: noun, adjective, verb, adverb.

You can use a thesaurus to:

- ▶ find a different word
- ▶ avoid repetition and clichés
- ▶ jog your memory over words you have forgotten.

It is easy to get drunk on new words and it can be tempting to use all the suggested words that fit. If you do find a word that you are unfamiliar with, look it up in your dictionary before using it. If you are not careful, you can end up using a word that does not quite fit the context. Use synonyms carefully and with restraint. You want your words to flow, not stutter along as you throw different and increasingly obscure words into your sentences. If you feel you are repeating yourself too much or are running out of synonyms, you should think about redrafting your proposed sentences.

Roget's is not the only thesaurus available. *Bartlett's Roget's Thesaurus* is an American version; Random House produces *Webster's College Thesaurus* for example. There are also various versions online. If you are going to use a thesaurus, check that you have got an up-to-date version.

Insight

You can be very creative with a thesaurus. Don't just look for direct substitutes. If you wanted to describe a heavy rainstorm or deluge, try looking for the exact opposite (dry, drought, parched) to see whether you can come up with a clever, striking alternative.

DICTIONARIES

Everyone should have a dictionary. They explain what words mean, how to spell them and whether a word is formal, slang or dialect. Dictionaries are records of a language in use at a particular time.

A monolingual dictionary just deals with one language (rather than a French – English dictionary, for example, which gives the meaning of a word in a different language). There are four basic categories of monolingual dictionary:

- ▶ Historical: traces the development of words (like the Oxford English Dictionary).

- Synchronic: language being used at the current time (like the Collins Concise Dictionary).
- Varieties/dialects of language – like the Dictionary of South African English or Dictionary of English – Scottish.
- Special aspect of a language – such as dialect or slang.

If you use a dictionary, you can learn a lot about each word including:

- the part of speech
- pronunciation
- definitions of the world, listed in order of importance
- some common expressions using the word
- other forms of the word
- something about the history of the word.
- whether it is acceptable in formal English.

> ### Did you know?
> The Oxford University Press has a vault of 'non words' that have not made it into the *Oxford English Dictionary*. Words include 'earworm': a catchy tune that you can't get out of your head; 'Sprog': to go slower than a sprint but faster than a jog; 'Furgle': to feel around in your pocket for a coin or key.

Be aware that one dictionary can be very different from another. The choice of words listed can vary as can the points of usage and even spelling. If you are going to use a dictionary at work, make sure your colleagues use the same one (and the most recent version) to avoid inconsistencies. You can obviously look up words on the internet but it is always useful to have a book on your shelf, near at hand. When buying a dictionary:

- Make sure it is up-to-date; look inside at the reverse title page to see when it was published or revised.
- Does it list the kind of words you will want to use?
- How does it explain the meanings of words? Some dictionaries go into great detail while others are more concise. Pick one that suits your needs.
- Does it give examples of word usage? That can be helpful, especially with unfamiliar words.
- Is it easy to understand how to pronounce the words?

- ▶ If you want slang and idiom, check that they are included in the definitions; not every dictionary lists them.
- ▶ Is it a well-made, robust book that is easy to read?

Insight

It is a good idea to try to learn a new word or two each week. Make sure that they are words you can use and not so obscure that most people will be unfamiliar with them. When you read other people's work, look for words that you don't know. Make a note of them and learn them.

Style manuals

Major institutions, like newspapers, have style manuals that list that particular institution's preference for punctuation, capitalization, and abbreviations and so on. Some of the better known are *The Chicago Manual of Style, The Times Style and Usage Guide, The Associated Press Stylebook* and *The Economist Style Guide*.

If you want to know what *The Economist* does with hyphens, for example, you can check it in the *Style Guide* ('Do not use a hyphen in place of *to* except with figures'). While *The Guardian*'s style guide says hyphens 'tend to clutter up text'.

These manuals are published and available to anyone. You can adopt one of these styles as your own or develop your own particular style if you wish. As discussed in Chapter 6, you can always compile your own editorial style guide.

Writing myths

As well as legitimate rules of grammar and punctuation, many myths about what is – and is not – acceptable have grown up over the years. Some of the more common myths are discussed here; there are further examples in the Appendix.

STARTING A SENTENCE WITH 'AND, BUT, BECAUSE, SO, HOWEVER...'

Why not? There is no rule that says you cannot start a sentence with these conjunctions. It is perfectly acceptable in conversation and informal writing. But if overused it can become irritating. For example:

▶ She declared she would run the marathon. Or maybe swim the Channel.

Using 'or' here suggests indecision on the part of the subject of the sentence.

▶ It was a good idea. But not everyone was happy.

Using 'but' at the beginning of a sentence emphasizes the point being made

Some commentators (such as Strunk & White) have said a sentence should not begin with 'however' when it means 'nevertheless' but that is only their opinion. You can use 'however' at the start of a sentence; you just need to know where to put the comma. If you don't use, you change the meaning of the word into 'in whatever manner' or 'to whatever extent'. For example, there are subtle differences to these two phrases:

▶ However, we tried to apply online.
▶ However we tried to apply online.

ENDING A SENTENCE WITH A PREPOSITION

What are you on *about*? What is the world coming *to*? Yes, of course you can end a sentence with a preposition, such as 'to', 'in', 'on', 'with' or 'about'. The rule goes back to Latin, where ending a sentence with a preposition was wrong. Trying to avoid putting a preposition at the end can end up with a very clumsy sentence. Winston Churchill thought it was a silly rule; he famously wrote, 'This is the sort of English up with I shall not put.'

▶ Tell me about whom he spoke.
▶ Tell me whom he spoke about.

Both of the above examples are correct; the first one is the more grammatically acceptable but it sounds very stuffy and formal; the second phrase is much closer to how we would speak.

NONE

Many people believe that the word 'none' is a contraction of 'not one', making it singular. However, 'none' can also mean 'not any' which is plural. So, if you are using it in the first context (none = not one, no amount) make sure it has a singular verb and, with the second context, use a plural verb. Just be consistent.

PUT THE SUBJECT BEFORE THE VERB

We have looked at this in earlier chapters but let's repeat it again here. While the traditional and more common sequence of a sentence is 'subject – verb – object', it is perfectly acceptable to change the sequence now and again.

SPLIT INFINITIVES

The infinitive describes verbs that do not have a subject: 'to drink', 'to go', 'to be' are all infinitives. To split an infinitive means to put a word in between 'to' and the verb: 'to boldly go' is perhaps the most famous split infinitive of the twentieth century.

You *can* split infinitives in English; you cannot in Latin which is where this rule came from. In Latin, an infinitive is a single word ('amare') while in English it is two ('to love'). At some point in the past, someone decreed that English infinitives should never be split either.

The only time you should avoid splitting an infinitive is when it changes the meaning. Look at the following two sentences. While all the words used in the sentence are the same, the meaning is slightly different in each:

▶ Jo decided to quickly clean her room.
▶ Jo decided quickly to clean her room.

To split or not to split is a matter of style and preference. 'To boldly go' sounds fine and certainly no worse than 'to go boldly' or 'boldly to go'. Most adverbs can be moved around the sentence without losing the sense and keeping the rhythm. Make sure your sentences flow and *sound* right, rather than worry whether you have split an infinitive or not.

NOUNS INTO VERBS

There is a tendency to turn nouns into verbs, especially in American English. It is not a new development but there has been an increase in these kind of words. A book is 'authored' rather than written, pupils are 'tasked' to write essays and even nouns are 'verbed'.

Some purists dislike this trend, while others argue that it is just another example of a living language, adapting and changing. Using a noun as a verb usually works best when something new appears, such as a new process or technology. The verb 'to text' is widely used, as is the noun 'a text'; both help give clarity to the language.

IT IS I

Grammatically, this is correct. The subject, I, comes after the verb 'to be'. However, this can sound quite old-fashioned and stuffy. Most of us do not speak like this (we are more likely to say 'it was me') and it can therefore sound odd in informal writing.

This also applies to phrases such as 'That's her', 'it's him' and 'me too' (which are the more commonly used, everyday way of speaking and writing) rather than the grammatically correct but awkwardly sounding 'that's she', 'it's he' and 'I too'.

ALRIGHT – ALL RIGHT

'Alright' is first recorded in 1893 and it has become popular, especially in informal writing, and the word is recognized in some dictionaries. It is personal preference or matter of style whether you use the one word or two.

However, many regard 'alright' as unacceptable. In *Modern English Usage*, Fowler writes, 'The use of 'all right', or [the] inability to see that there is anything wrong with 'alright', reveals one's background, upbringing, education, etc., perhaps as much as any word in the language.' Or, as the saying goes, 'alright is always all wrong'. So it is best avoided if you do not want to offend anyone – certainly if you are writing formally.

WILL VS SHALL

A lot of grammar and style books have got quite animated about when 'will' and 'shall' should be used, insisting that there is a clear distinction between the two. However, that distinction seems to be blurring, if not disappearing. In the *New Oxford Dictionary of English*, it says 'shall' and 'will' can be used interchangeably. 'Will' seems to be more commonly used than 'shall' so it seems perfectly acceptable to use it. 'Shall' is useful if you want to imply or show power by the person using it; for example, 'you shall go to the ball' is someone making a promise, while 'you shall not be allowed out' is more of an order or threat.

For those, though, that would like to know the difference between the two:

- If you want to express the future, use 'shall' if you are writing in the first person (I/we shall go) but use 'will' for the third person (you/s/he/they will go).
- If you want to express intention to act, use 'will' in the first person (we will go) and 'shall' in the third person (they shall go).

WHO AND WHOM

Both are pronouns. Many people are unsure of when to use 'whom' and tend to leave it out. The simple rule is that you use 'who' when you are referring to the subject of a clause and 'whom' when you are referring to the object. The rules that apply for 'who' and 'whom' also apply to 'whoever' and 'whomever'.

Insight

If you are not sure when to use 'whom', substitute 'him' (or 'her') into the sentence. If it makes sense, then you can use 'whom'. If it does not, use 'who'.

THAT, WHICH

These are two pronouns which can cause confusion. Writers are often unsure which one is the correct option to use in a sentence. Their role is that of a defining (that) or non-defining (which) clause.

- **Non-defining** – acts like a clause in parenthesis; in other words, it could be left out and the sentence would still make sense. It does not define the meaning of the sentence in that sense ('the frog, which was green and yellow, was from the Amazon).
- **Defining** – it is essential to the sentence; it gives it its meaning and defining characteristic ('The frog that was green and yellow is from the Amazon').

You can always avoid the problem by leaving the pronoun out of the sentence. For example, rather than worrying whether it should be 'the train *that* I was catching' or 'the train *which* I was catching', don't have a pronoun at all. The sense of the sentence remains the same: 'the train I was catching'.

Did you know?

There is a website (www.iwl.me) which analyses your word choice and writing style and compares it to those of famous writers. Just cut and paste some of your text onto the website to see whether you are the next Robert Louis Stevenson, Charles Dickens or Lewis Carroll.

Interviewing techniques

Good writing is always helped by strong facts and information. It is not only journalists that have to do their research and interview people for stories. Essays (school and college), reports, any form of non-fiction, in fact, could include information gathered from an interview. To do this effectively, you need to improve your interviewing technique.

Interviewing is not the same as having a conversation. It can certainly help the interview if your 'subject' feels as if they are having a chat but, as the interviewer, you have a job to do.

A good interviewer will not show off; it is not about how much you know but more about getting the interviewee to explain what they know, in their own words.

▶ Do research your topic and your interviewee so you are prepared.
▶ Keep your interviewee relaxed; don't put them on the defensive.
▶ Avoid asking leading questions; you may be after certain information but don't try to put words in their mouth.
▶ Your last question should always be 'Is there anything I haven't asked you that you would like to mention?'

Adding colour

George Orwell wrote that you should 'never use a metaphor, simile or other figure of speech which you are used to seeing in print'. He is referring to clichéd phrases (like 'pure as the driven snow', 'blue sky thinking'). He was right to object to writers reusing tired phrases but figures of speech and word play in general can give colour and energy to a piece of writing. Without them, writing can seem dull and lifeless.

Wordplay can make your writing memorable, attention grabbing, lively, moving and thought-provoking. Use wordplay to drive a message home; not show off for the sake of it. The following are some examples of how you can brighten up your writing:

ALLITERATION

A repetition of the same sounds of words ('Sing a song of sixpence', 'Peter picked a peck of pickled peppers'), it gives writing a strong rhythm and can drive home an idea in the reader's mind.

CONVERSION

This is where a noun, verb or adjective is turned into something different (see 'Nouns into verbs' above). For example, 'She's been DJ-ing in Ibiza'. A DJ is a noun; here it has been turned into an adjective. Use to take a well-known expression or word and turn it on its head.

EUPHEMISM

A euphemism is a vague or more favourable expression used as a substitute for the more accurate (but indelicate or blunt) description; used when you want to avoid making a direct statement – often because you do not want to offend or hurt someone's feelings, e.g. 'hard of hearing' rather than 'deaf'. Euphemisms are used when talking about death, sex and bodily functions, e.g. 'he passed away', 'making the beast with two backs', 'spending a penny'.

HYPERBOLE

This is a deliberate exaggeration ('We're starving and dying of thirst') to make a point. 'Litotes' is the opposite of hyperbole; it means an understatement.

SIMILE

Compares one thing with another; uses 'like' or 'as' to link the two together. For example, 'as white as snow', 'mad as a snake', 'her sharp tongue cut me like a knife', 'we took to dancing like ducks to water'. As with metaphors, there are a lot of very tired, clichéd similes so it is always a good idea to try to come up with your own simile rather than reuse an old familiar one.

METAPHOR

Lynn Truss in her book on punctuation, *Eats, Shoots and Leaves*, uses a wonderful metaphor when describing commas:

> **[The comma evolved into] a kind of scary grammatical sheepdog... [that] tears about the hillside of language, endlessly organising words into sensible groups.'**

Similar to a simile, a metaphor compares things as if they are identical or substitutes for one another. Used heavily in fiction and poetry, English is full of every day metaphors. We all use them, perhaps without realizing it; we talk of 'the mouth of the river' and 'being over the moon'. Rivers do not possess actual mouths; very few of us have been over or around the moon.

Metaphors brighten up writing, making words memorable and interesting; they can illustrate a difficult idea or concept. Many metaphors have passed into everyday speech (such as the 'the train journey was a nightmare') while others have become clichéd and tired ('opening a can of worms') because they have been overused. You can invent your own metaphors but beware of getting carried away by them (know when to stop) or mixing them.

METONYMY

This is where the name of one thing or concept is applied to something it is closely associated with. When we talk about 'the crown', we actually mean the monarch or royalty; 'the bottle' can mean strong drink; we count 'heads' rather than people.

NEOLOGISM

These are new word formations. Shakespeare is believed to have come up with around 1500 new words (including 'grovel' and 'puke'). In more recent times, Orwell created 'newspeak' and JK Rowling 'muggles'. Corporate businesses are also known for making up new words (like 'tweeting') and anyone at the forefront of a cultural or social movement usually creates a few new words ('metrosexual', 'affluenza'). Neologism can either be newly created single words or combinations of existing words ('eco-warrior').

ONOMATOPOEIA

These are words that are formed from a sound associated with what is being named. Examples are: 'splat', 'ker-ching', 'moo', 'plop', 'fizz'.

OXYMORON

An oxymoron is a figure of speech or phrase that combines two normally contradictory terms ('common delicacy', 'disgustingly delicious') to create a startling or surprising phrase. Use oxymoron if you want to emphasize something, be sarcastic or arch. They work well in speeches too.

PERSONIFICATION

Personification occurs when representing an object as a person, such as talking about your car as a living creature ('she was running beautifully until she got a flat tyre'; 'the rock sat there, looking menacing, daring him to pick it up').

REPETITION

Not all repetition is bad. It has its place in writing; poetry relies heavily on repetition of key words and sentence patterns. And it works well in fiction too. Repetition can make a point more memorable or give added emphasis. Winston Churchill used repetition to great effect, '...we shall fight on the beaches, we shall fight on the landing grounds, we shall fight in the fields and in the streets, we shall fight in the hills...' as did Abraham Lincoln ('government of the people, by the people, for the people'). But this kind of repetition has to be planned carefully to get the required effect.

Unplanned repetition can be a distraction, hampering understanding and comprehension. If the reader thinks poorly of the writer, they are not going to trust what they are saying. There are areas where it should be avoided:

▶ Inadvertently rhyming – 'He's a poet and we know it'.
▶ Unintended alliteration (repetition of a particular sound or letter) – 'Staff in strategic roles should establish standards'.
▶ Same word repeated in the sentence ('The word needs to be put between words of more than one syllable'.

On that last point, there are times when you have to use the same word or phrase more than once. Yes, it can be dull if you continue to use the same word and go on using the same word but sometimes it would be more complicated, confusing and awkward to try to substitute different words.

Insight
Don't worry about repeating 'said' when you are writing dialogue. It is preferable to have repetition of that word, rather than raid your thesaurus and have your speaker comment, ponder, reason, opine, whisper, chuckle and fume.

Put it before them briefly so they will read it, clearly so they will appreciate it, picturesquely so they will remember it and, above all, accurately so they will be guided by its light.

Joseph Pulitzer

Tools of the trade

We all have tools of our trade to help us do our jobs; chefs have their knives, builders have their hammers and chisels, doctors their stethoscopes. When you write, you need to have the correct tools.

▶ Always have something to hand to write on; you never know when inspiration may strike.
▶ If you are writing on a computer, back up your work!
▶ Make sure your virus protection is up to date.

Create the right environment so you can be effective when writing. It is not easy if you are answering the phone all the time, colleagues or friends are dropping in and interrupting or the children want attention. You want to be comfortable and not distracted. Whether you are writing at home or at work, let people know that you are not to be disturbed during your 'writing time'.

Make sure you have everything you need close at hand (paper, pens, pencils, dictionaries, reference books, etc.). If you have to stop and go and look for something, it can interrupt the flow and make it hard to get going again.

If you spend long hours at your desk, working on your computer, make sure your work station is set up to help protect your back, neck and arms.

▶ Your arms should be at a relaxed 90-degree angle.
▶ The top of the monitor screen should be at eye level.
▶ The monitor should be at arms-length.
▶ Your feet should be flat on the floor.

Writer's block

Some days the words just don't want to come out. You know you should start putting words down but you are not sure which ones and where to start. All writers have problems getting started, even the professionals. Ernest Hemingway said that one of the most frightening things he ever encountered was 'A blank sheet of paper'; while William Goldman said 'The easiest thing to do on earth is not write.'

If you can, write a draft as soon as possible, rather than spend lots of time researching. You will find out what information you are missing once you put the draft down on paper. The sooner you actually start writing the better. The longer you put off writing, the harder it is to start.

Insight

Take a piece of paper or an empty screen and just start writing. It can be related to what you are supposed to be working on or it can just be a stream of thought. This is called 'free writing'. The important thing is to get words down. Look on it as a kind of warming up, a stretching of the writing muscles. Try not to think about it too much or edit it as you go along. Do this for five minutes or until you have filled three pages of A4.

Any writing practice is good practice. And it is easy to do. You don't need to be at your computer. You can take a notebook and pencil and scribble a few thoughts down, sitting at your desk, sitting on the train or sitting in a cafe.

Remember that it is highly unlikely that your first draft will be the final one. The best writers work on their words; they polish, tweak, change, rewrite huge chunks and sometimes start from scratch. It is also why great writers have great editors; to help them make their words even better. Don't be hard on yourself when it comes to writing. It is a craft and you have to work on it.

WAYS OF DEALING WITH WRITER'S BLOCK

▶ Consider what you have to write. Write down a few questions and then leave them for a few hours (ideally overnight or a couple of days). Don't think about the questions or the problems you are having. Then go back to the questions and write down the first things that come into your head. Very often this can produce the answers you were looking for.
▶ Rewrite the last page (or paragraph) to pick up momentum again.
▶ Go and do something productive, even if it just the ironing or sorting out your sock drawer; a change of focus can take the pressure off and the sense of achievement that you get from actually doing something can kick start your writing.
▶ Move – go and write somewhere else; a change of scenery can be stimulating.

- ▶ Jump about – on the page. If you are having trouble starting a piece, ignore the opening sentence or paragraph, find a bit that you can write. It could be somewhere in the middle, the conclusion, anywhere.
- ▶ Jump about – between different projects. If you have got several writing projects, leave the one that is giving you trouble and go and do another one (a letter to a friend, a business email, your diary).
- ▶ Set yourself a target of writing for a set period of time. When you have met that target...
- ▶ Reward yourself. Let yourself have a cup of tea and a biscuit when you've written the first draft or go for a quick walk when you have finished the second page.

Being a writer

Whether you write for pleasure or because it is part of your job, you have to practise a bit of discipline. You need to give yourself some structure in order to function effectively when you write. Be ruthless with yourself and your time.

- ▶ Find a place where you can write. It does not have to be at a desk; if you find you are most creative on a dining table, the garden shed or the cafeteria, then go and write there. Scott Thurow wrote Presumed Innocent on his daily commute to work on the train; JK Rowling famously wrote Harry Potter in an Edinburgh café.
- ▶ Work out when you can write. All writers, whether they are best-selling novelists, students or writing an annual report, have an optimum time of day which suits them and they can write well. Make sure you take advantage of that time.
- ▶ If you can't choose a time to write, experiment to find out when you are at your most creative and able to give some thought and attention to what you have to write. If you get the time right, you can be really productive in a relatively short space of time.
- ▶ Keep practising at writing (write letters to friends, an article for the parish magazine, a short review of a play or a television programme); think of it as exercising, keeping your writing muscles in trim.

English – an exciting and evolving language

Good writing is a skill and one that takes practice. Even the greatest writers have to work at their writing. This book will help you with that.

In every generation, there is a school of thought that laments the decline in English. There have been dire warnings on the state of the language since the sixteenth century but we are still managing to write and communicate. Some of the doomsayers worry because they believe the only right way is to stick to rules that must never change. But all living languages change and develop. They have to. As new technologies are created, foreign influences appear and social changes come about, the language evolves to accommodate them.

We do not want English to stop changing. What we do want is to be able to express ourselves clearly. One of the strengths of the English language is its adaptability; it can be used in so many ways. That is also its weakness because confusion and ambiguity are never far away if the language is used carelessly. It is not so much rules that govern us but convention. We stick to convention in English and grammar because it is practical to do so; we want the people we are communicating with to understand us so it makes sense to abide by those recognizable conventions. A few rules and conventions keep our writing easy to understand.

10 THINGS TO TRY

1 Write down a list of clichéd metaphors ('red as a rose', 'white as snow', etc.) and come up with some new alternatives.

2 Read books, newspapers and magazines; expose yourself to well-written English.

3 Review manuals of style.

4 Build your own reference library.

5 Aim to learn a new word each week; open a dictionary at random to find a new word. Try to incorporate it in your writing in the next few days.

6 Take three sheets of A4 paper and fill them. Write about anything but just fill the three pages. Do this each day.

7 Practise writing in a different context or style; if you always write emails and reports, try writing a short story or a news report.

8 Read the same news report but in different contexts (different newspapers, websites, etc.). Look at the differences between the writer's style. What works best?

9 Keep an eye out for good beginnings (in reports, letters, emails). What grabbed your attention? What did you like about them? What made them work? Build up a collection of good openings.

10 Make a note of any new words that you come across; learn them and try to use in your writing.

Appendix

Commonly misspelled words

Accidentally	not accidently
Accommodate	remember there are two m's
A lot	there is no such word as 'alot'. You can have 'a lot' of money or you can 'allot money to people'.
Barbecue	rather than barbeque
Besiege	not beseige
Dispensable	
Drunkenness	
Embarrass/embarrassment	there are two r's and two s's
Encumbrance	not encumberance
Exorbitant	not exhorbitant
Expatriate	not expatriot
Eyeing	with an 'i'
Feasible	
Flak	not flack
Ghettos	not ghettoes
Grievous	not grievious
Harass	not harrass
Inadmissible	
Incomprehensible	
Keenness	not keenness
Minuscule	means a small script or letter. It is frequently misspelt as 'miniscule'. Think of 'minus' rather than 'mini'.
Misspell	
Nerve-racking	not nerve-wracking
Potato/potatoes	
Sanitary	not sanitory
Salutary	
Staccato	

Subterranean	
Subtle/subtlety	
Suddenness	two d's, two n's, two s's
Superintendent	
Target/targeting/targeted	
Teammate	not teamate
Thief/thieves	
Thyme	when referring to the herb
Tomato/tomatoes	
Troop (army) / troupe (actors)	
Tunnel / tunnelling	but tunneling in American English
Veterinary / veterinarian	
Vocabulary	
Whisky (Scotch) / Whiskey (American or Irish)	
Withhold	two h's
Woollen/woolly (in the UK)	woolen/wooly (in the US)
Wrath	not rath/roth

Commonly misused words

Adverse – averse
Being 'adverse' to something means you are hostile to or against it; 'averse' means you are reluctant to do something.

Affected – effected
Affect: (verb) to influence (sometimes to pretend). To be affected is to be deeply moved. (noun) the way one relates to and shows emotion. Effect: (verb) to accomplish, bring about. (noun) the result of some action.

Alternate – alternative
'To alternate' (a verb) means to go back and forth between two things. 'Alternate' (adjective) means 'every other' and as a noun means to 'stand-in for' (someone else). 'Alternative', as a noun, can either mean a choice between one or two things, or more than two things; in other words, one or the other.

Amoral – immoral

'Amoral' is used when you are talking about things where the question of morality does not apply. 'Immoral' means not conforming to moral standards.

Anticipate

When you anticipate something, you look ahead to it and prepare for it: 'We anticipate some opposition to our plans so we will bring the matter to the Board at the next meeting.' 'Anticipate' is also being used to mean 'to expect or foresee': 'The meal was more enjoyable than anticipated.' This second meaning is frowned upon by some but it is acceptable. 'Anticipate' cannot mean 'expect as one's due', as in: 'I anticipate payment by the end of the week'; that is incorrect, it should be 'I expect...'.

Bad – badly

You feel bad if you do something wrong; you feel badly if you drink too much.

Between – among

The general rule is that if you are writing about two things or people, use 'between'; use 'among' when the amount/number is not clear. There are, of course, exceptions; it is more acceptable to write that 'Coventry is between Birmingham, Rugby, Warwick and Leicester' rather than 'among'.

Between you and I

It should be 'between you and me'

Biweekly/bimonthly

This continues to confuse people. Does 'biweekly' mean 'appearing twice a week', 'appearing twice weekly' or 'appearing every two weeks'? It is better to avoid using the prefix 'bi-' and state what you mean very clearly (fortnightly, every two years and so on).

Can/may

Use 'can' when something is possible ('you can take the next bus') and 'may' for something that is permissible: 'you may sit down'.

Chronic – acute

When talking about a disease or medical condition, chronic means 'long-lasting'; acute means a sudden attack or illness which needs immediate treatment.

Compare to – compare with
If you compare something *with* something else, you are pointing out the differences between the two. If you compare something *to* something else, you are showing how alike they are.

Compel – impel
Both can be used to suggest force being used to make something happen but they are slightly different. 'Compel' suggests a stronger pressure. 'Impel' describes a gentler, more encouraging force.

Complement – compliment
'Complement', with an 'e', means to make complete or whole. 'Compliment' is to praise or flatter.

Comprise – comprise of
'Comprise' means 'to contain', 'to be composed of' or 'consist of'. Nothing should ever be 'comprised of'; for example, 'A full pack comprises 52 cards' (Fowler, *Modern English Usage*).

Condone
It means to pardon, forgive or excuse. It does not mean to endorse or approve something.

Councillor – counsellor
The first is a member of a local government council. A counsellor is someone who gives advice (either legal advice, help with personal problems, etc.). 'Council' is also a noun; 'counsel' can be used as a verb (to give advice).

Defective – deficient
Use 'defective' for something that is not working properly. 'Deficient' means lacking something.

Defuse – diffuse
'Defuse' means literally to remove a fuse (as in an explosive device) and can also be used to mean removing tension or danger. 'Diffuse' means disperse or distribute widely.

Different from – different to
'Different from' is the usual form ('girls are different from boys'), especially when 'from' is in front of a noun or pronoun.

Disassemble – dissemble
You disassemble when you take something apart. You are concealing something if you dissemble.

Discreet – discrete
The first means unobtrusive ('a discreet dab of perfume') while the second means individually distinct or unattached.

Each other – one another
Use 'each other' when you are talking about two people/things; if there are three or more, use 'one another'.

Elder – older
'Elder' is an adjective which you use when describing who is the oldest of two people ('My elder sister'). It is a noun to describe a respected member of a community; it is also a tree. 'Older' (and 'oldest') just means more old.

Enquire – inquire
There is no great distinction between the two so it is up to personal preference which one you use.

Every day – everyday
'Everyday' is an adjective, for example: 'everyday event', 'everyday mention'). If the meaning is 'each day', then use two words: 'they went swimming nearly every day.'

Farther – further
Farther – a longer distance away. Generally used with literal distances ('I live farther from my mother than my sister does'). Further – more or additional; a figurative distance ('I can go no further').

Good – well
'Good' is an adjective; 'well' is an adverb (unless you are talking about your health).

▶ Did you enjoy the play? Was it any good? ('good' describes 'it' – adjective)
▶ Kate ran well ('well' describes the running – adverb).

Great Britain – United Kingdom
Great Britain is the collective name for England, Scotland and Wales. The United Kingdom includes Great Britain and Northern Ireland.

Hanged – hung
The old saying 'People are hanged; pictures are hung' is a useful way to remember correct usage here.

If – whether
Both connect one idea to another in a sentence but should be used in different contexts. 'If' describes a possibility: 'If we take the left turn, we will see the church.' 'Whether' should be used when choosing between two options, as in 'whether or not': 'We did not know whether to take the left turn to find the church'.

Imply – infer
You 'suggest' or 'hint' at something when you 'imply'; you 'deduce' when you 'infer'.

In to – into
If the action being described ends up with the subject within the object, use *into* ('We got into the car'); if it does not, use *in to* (He walked in to a wall).

Iterate – reiterate
Both mean the same thing: to repeat.

Lend – loan
'Lend' is a verb, while 'loan' is a noun; the bank *lends* you money; you now have a *loan* from the bank. However, 'loan' is increasingly used as a verb.

Less – fewer
'Less' (meaning 'not as much') applies to quantities that cannot be counted; mass nouns such as 'sugar', 'energy', 'anger' or 'power'. Use 'few' and 'fewer' ('not as many') when referring to countable nouns (that have singular and plural forms) and collective nouns; such as 'people', 'chairs', 'audience'.

Did you know?
Tesco removed signs that read 'Ten items or less' in 2008 and replaced them with 'Up to 10 items' following pressure from people who knew their grammar.

Loath – loathe
'Loath' (without an 'e' and pronounced with a soft 'th' sound) means to be reluctant or averse to something: 'We were loath to leave the beach'). 'Loathe' means 'to hate': 'They loathed their new teacher.'

Naval – navel
The first (with an 'a') means anything to do with the navy; the second (with an 'e') is your belly button.

Neither – none
'Neither' is singular if it refers to a pair of individual people or things; use it in the plural if you are referring to a pair of groups. 'None' is a pronoun that has traditionally taken the singular format (the word comes from 'not one'). However, most dictionaries say that it is quite common to see it used as a plural. 'None of us is going' is grammatically correct but sounds awkward to modern ears; 'none of us are going' is more acceptable.

On to – onto
'Onto' began appearing in the twentieth century. It is now firmly established in American English and becoming more common in British English. 'Onto' is used as a compound preposition ('We rushed onto the train') and 'on to' when 'on' is an adverb ('The teacher moved on to the next book').

Oral – aural
They are pronounced the same in British English but have different meanings. 'Oral' means 'by mouth'; medicine can be taken orally, an oral statement is one that is spoken. 'Aural' is related to the ear or hearing ('an aural examination').

Pore – pour
'I pore over the map' means I look at the map closely; 'I pour the coffee' (meaning allowing a stream of liquid to flow).

Practice – practise
The noun has 'c'; while the verb, 'to practise' is spelled with an 's'. The same goes for 'advice/advise'. To help you remember, 'n' (for 'noun') comes before 'v' (for 'verb') in the alphabet; 'c' comes before 's' in the alphabet. Unless you are American and then you do not have to worry about this (see Chapter 5).

Prescribe – proscribe
To 'prescribe' is to recommend, to lay down a course to be followed or to issue a medical prescription. To 'proscribe' is to forbid, reject or condemn something.

Principal – principle
'Principal' can be an adjective (meaning first in rank) or a noun (meaning someone who is the head of something, superior to others). 'Principle' is a noun which means fundamental truth or law: 'the principles of reason'.

Program – programme
The first is the standard American spelling; while British English uses the '-amme' ending – except when referring to anything related to computers. Then, the spelling is 'program' (meaning a sequence of instructions for a computer).

Prostate – prostrate
The first is a noun; it is a gland found in male mammals. 'Prostrate' (with a second 'r') means literally lying face down but is also used to mean overcome with grief or exhaustion.

Rise – raise
'Rise' – to stand or get up. It is a self-contained action. The subject 'does' the action to themselves (i.e. they rise, nobody else does it for them). 'Raise' is to lift something or someone else. The action starts with one person/thing and then moves to another: 'We raised the cup.'

Stationary – stationery
With an 'a' (stationary), the word means to be still or stand still. Spelt with an 'e', 'stationery' means paper, envelopes, notepads, etc.

That – who
Generally, you use 'that' when writing about anyone and 'who' when you are writing about a particular person:

▶ The dancers that performed last night.
▶ The shop assistant who helped me.

To – too – two
They all sound alike but are spelled differently and have different meanings. *To* can be part of the infinitive of a verb (to read, to listen)

or show movement: 'We're going to the zoo'. *Two* is a number; *too* means 'as well, more than enough, also'.

Venal – venial
They look very similar but the two words have very different meanings. 'Venal' means 'can be bought', 'for sale', 'corruptly mercenary'. 'Venial' means 'pardonable' or 'excusable' (a venial sin can be forgiven, for example).

Wreath – wreathe
A 'wreath' is a circlet made of intertwined materials, like flowers, and is a noun; 'wreathe' is a verb and means intertwining or twisted together.

Wreak – reek
The first is a verb meaning to drive out, give expression to ('wreak vengeance' or 'wreak havoc'); the second can be a noun or verb and relates to a strong unpleasant smell ('the reek of rotting meat').

Taking it further

USEFUL PUBLICATIONS

Note: Many of these titles are updated into new editions frequently, therefore the year of publication has not necessarily been included.

Amis, Kingsley, *The King's English* (Penguin Classics, 1998)

The Associated Press Stylebook (Basic Books)

Austin, Tim (editor), *The Times Style and Usage Guide* (Times Books)

Bryson, Bill, *Troublesome Words* (Penguin, 2009)

Carr, Nicholas, *The Shallows: How the Internet Is Changing the Way We Think, Read and Remember* (Atlantic, 2010)

The Chicago Manual of Style (University of Chicago Press)

The Economist Style Guide (Economist Books)

Fowler, H.W. & F.G., *The King's English* (Oxford University Press, 2002)

Garner, Bryan, *Garner's Modern American Usage* (USA: Oxford University Press)

New Hart's Rules: The Handbook of Style for Writers and Editors (Oxford: Oxford University Press)

Oxford Dictionary of Foreign words & Phrases (Oxford Paperback Reference)

Palmer, Frank, *Grammar* (Penguin, 1971)

Partridge, Eric, *Usage & Abusage: A Guide to Good English* (Penguin, 2005)

Plotnik, Arthur, *Spunk & Bite: A Writer's Guide to Punchier, More Engaging Language & Style* (Random House, 2005)

Strunk Jr, William & White E.B., *The Elements of Style* (Longman)

Fowler's Modern English Usage (Oxford: Oxford University Press)

The New York Times Manual of Style and Usage (Crown Publishers)

Truss, Lynn, *Eats, Shoots and Leave: The Zero Tolerance Approach to Punctuation* (Profile Books, 2003)

USEFUL TEACH YOURSELF BOOKS (HODDER EDUCATION)

Get That Job with the Right CV

Improve Your Copywriting

Improve Your Handwriting

Improve Your Spelling

Make a Great Speech

Write Great Essays and Dissertations

DICTIONARIES

The American Heritage Dictionary (Delta)

Collins Plain English Dictionary (Collins)

Concise Oxford English Dictionary (Oxford University Press)

The Chambers Dictionary (Chambers, Hodder Education)

The New Oxford Dictionary for Writers and Editors (Oxford University Press)

Oxford English Dictionary, Second Edition (Clarendon Press)

Webster's International Dictionary (Merriam Webster)

THESAURUS

Bartlett's Roget's Thesaurus (Little, Brown & Company)

Random House Webster's College Thesaurus (Random House Reference Publishing)

Roget's Super Thesaurus (Writer's Digest Books)

Roget's International Thesaurus (Collins Reference)

Roget's 21st Century Thesaurus in Dictionary Form (Bantam Doubleday Dell)

American Copy Editors Society: www.copydesk.org

Debrett's Online: www.debretts.com

Dictionary & thesaurus: www.merriam-webster.com

Emily Post: www.emilypost.com

Social media trends & information: www.mashable.com

Write like a famous author? Go to www.iwl.me

Jargon buster: http://oxforddictionaries.com/page/jargonbuster/jargon-buster

BBC Grammar Guide, a quick reference guide to grammatical terms: www.bbc.co.uk/skillswise/words/grammar

Online Thesaurus: www.wordsmyth.net

Oxford English Dictionary: www.oed.com

Plain language (US Federal Govt): www.plainlanguage.gov

Visual thesaurus that creates word maps: www.visualthesaurus.com

www.problogger.net

www.copyblogger.com

ORGANIZATIONS

The Apostrophe Protection Society
Aims to preserve the correct use of 'this currently much abused punctuation mark in all forms of text written in the English language'.

www.apostrophe.org.uk
23 Vauxhall Road
Boston
Lincolnshire PE21 0JB
E: chairman@apostrophe.org.uk

National Institute of Adult Continuing Education (NIACE)
www.niace.org.uk

Aims to encourage all adults to engage in learning of all kinds.

20 Princess Road West
Leicester LE1 6TP
T: 0116 204 4200
E: enquiries@niace.org.uk

National Literacy Trust
www.literacytrust.org

Supports those who struggle with literacy and the people who work with them.

68 South Lambeth Road
London SW8 1RL
E: support@literacytrust.org.uk

Plain English Campaign
www.plainenglish.co.uk

Campaigns against jargon, gobbledygook and misleading public information. The organization also issues the Crystal Mark, Internet Crystal Mark and Honesty Mark.

PO Box 3
New Mills
High Peak SK22 4QP
T: 01663 744409
F: 01663 747038
E: info@plainenglish.co.uk

ProLiteracy
www.proliteracy.org

Champions the power of literacy to improve the lives of adults and their families.

1320 Jamesville Ave.Syracuse, NY 13210
T: (315) 422 9121
Toll free: 1 888 528 2224
E: info@proliteracy.org

Queen's English Society
www.queens-english-society.com

British charity concerned about the decline in standards in the use of English.

Society for the Promotion of Good Grammar
http://spogg.org

The Society for the Preservation of Semicolon
On Facebook

World Wide Web Consortium (W3C)
www.w3.org

Issues standards and accessibility guidelines for websites.

National Grammar Day (US)
www.nationalgrammarday.com

Celebrated on 4 March. Founded by Martha Brockenbrough, founder of the Society for the Promotion of Good Grammar.

National Punctuation Day (US)
www.nationalpunctuationday.com

LITERARY CONSULTANCIES

Cornerstones Literary Agency
www.cornerstones.co.uk

Milk Studios
34 Southern Row
London W10 5AN
T: 020 8968 0777
E: Helen@cornerstones.co.uk/kathryn@cornerstones.co.uk

Hilary Johnson Authors' Advisory Service
www.hilaryjohnson.demon.co.uk

1 Beechwood Court
Syderstone
Norfolk PE31 8TR
T: 01485 578594
E: enquiries@hilaryjohnson.com

The Literary Consultancy
www.literaryconsultancy.co.uk

Free World Centre
60 Farringdon Road
London EC1R 3GA
T: 020 7324 2563
E: info@literaryconsultancy.co.uk

The Writer's Journey
www.juliamccutchen.com

PO Box 3703
Trowbridge BA14 6ZW
T: 01380 871331
E: Julia@juliamccutchen.com

Index

Image credits